AMERICA'S WARS THROUGH PRIMARY SOURCES

Primary Source Accounts of

World War I

DISCARD

GLENN SCHERER AND MARTY FLETCHER

MyReportLinks.com Books

an imprint of

Enslow Publishers, Inc. E

Box 398, 40 Industrial Road
Berkeley Heights, NJ 07922
USA

MyReportLinks.com Books, an imprint of Enslow Publishers, Inc. MyReportLinks®
is a registered trademark of Enslow Publishers, Inc.

Library of Congress Cataloging-in-Publication Data

Scherer, Glenn.
  Primary source accounts of World War I / Glenn Scherer and Marty Fletcher.
      p. cm. — (America's wars through primary sources)
  Includes bibliographical references and index.
  ISBN 1-59845-008-5
  1. World War, 1914–1918—Sources—Juvenile literature. I. Fletcher, Marty. II. Title. III. Series.
  D522.7.S44 2006
  940.3—dc22
                              2005028368

Printed in the United States of America

10 9 8 7 6 5 4 3 2 1

To Our Readers:
Through the purchase of this book, you and your library gain access to the Report Links that specifically back up this book.

The Publisher will provide access to the Report Links that back up this book and will keep these Report Links up to date on **www.myreportlinks.com** for five years from the book's first publication date.

We have done our best to make sure all Internet addresses in this book were active and appropriate when we went to press. However, the author and the Publisher have no control over, and assume no liability for, the material available on those Internet sites or on other Web sites they may link to.

The usage of the MyReportLinks.com Books Web site is subject to the terms and conditions stated on the Usage Policy Statement on **www.myreportlinks.com.**

A password may be required to access the Report Links that back up this book. The password is found on the bottom of page 4 of this book.

Any comments or suggestions can be sent by e-mail to comments@myreportlinks.com or to the address on the back cover.

Photo Credits: BBC, p. 25; Brigham Young University, p. 20; *Daily Herald,* London, England, p. 111; Duke University, p. 81; Emory University, p. 89; Enslow Publishers, Inc., pp. 8, 11; Georgetown University, p. 101; Library of Congress, pp. 3, 13, 15, 33, 38, 42–43, 47, 51, 55, 69, 74, 76, 77, 82, 85, 95, 97, 107; MyReportLinks.com Books, p. 4; National Archives and Records Administration, pp. 1, 10, 17, 37, 39, 40, 56, 78, 87; National Archives, United Kingdom, pp. 28–29, 58; PBS, p. 21; Smithsonian Institution, National Museum of American History, p. 49; The Aerodrome, p. 61; The Avalon Project at Yale Law School, p. 109; The Gilder Lehrman Institute of American History, p. 67; The History Channel, p. 53; The Veterans History Project, The Library of Congress, p. 35; Tutt Library, Colorado College, pp. 71, 102; U.S. Centennial of Flight Commission, p. 27; United States Military Academy, pp. 23, 41; University of North Carolina, p. 63; Veterans Museum and Memorial Center, p. 110.

Cover Photo: National Archives and Records Administration/U.S. Department of Defense.

Every effort has been made to locate all copyright holders of material used in this book. If any errors or omissions have occurred, please contact us at www.myreportlinks.com. We will try to make corrections in future editions.

CONTENTS

MyReportLinks.com Books
Great Books, Great Links, Great for Research!

The Internet sites featured in this book can save you hours of research time. These Internet sites—we call them **"Report Links"**—are constantly changing, but we keep them up to date on our Web site.

When you see this "Approved Web Site" logo, you will know that we are directing you to a great Internet site that will help you with your research.

Give it a try! Type http://www.myreportlinks.com into your browser, click on the series title and enter the password, then click on the book title, and scroll down to the Report Links listed for this book.

The Report Links will bring you to great source documents, photographs, and illustrations. MyReportLinks.com Books save you time, feature Report Links that are kept up to date, and make report writing easier than ever! A complete listing of the Report Links can be found on pages 112–113 at the back of the book.

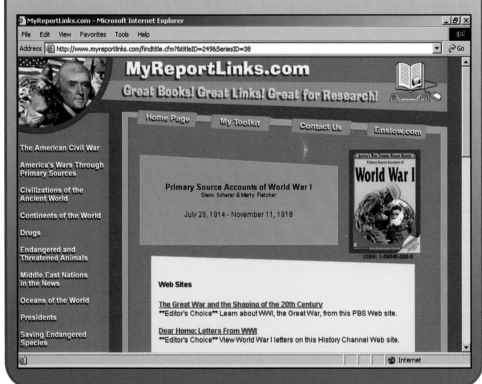

Please see "To Our Readers" on the copyright page for important information about this book, the MyReportLinks.com Web site, and the Report Links that back up this book.

Please enter **PWO1008** if asked for a password.

WHAT ARE PRIMARY SOURCES?

I got several breathes of the strong [poison gas] solution right from the shell before it got diluted with much air. If it hadn't been for the fellow with me I probably wouldn't be writing this letter because I couldn't see, . . . I gasped, choked and felt the extreme terror of the man who goes under in the water and will clutch at a straw.

—Doughboy Stull Holt in a letter to his family.

The young Marine who wrote these words never dreamed that they would be read by anyone but his wife. They were not intended to be read as a history of the First World War. But his words—and the words of others that have come down to us through scholars or were saved over generations by family members—are unique resources. Historians call such writings primary source documents. As you read this book, you will find other primary source accounts of the war written by the men and women who fought it. Their letters home reflect their thoughts, their dreams, their fears, and their longing for loved ones. Some of them speak of the excitement of battle, while others mention the everyday boredom of day-to-day life in camp.

But the story of a war is not only the story of the men and women in service. This book also contains diary entries, newspaper accounts, official documents, speeches, and songs of the war years. They reflect the opinions of those who were not in battle but who were still affected by the war. All of these things as well as photographs and art can be considered primary sources—they were created by people who participated in, witnessed, or were affected by the events of the time.

Many of these sources, such as letters and diaries, are a reflection of personal experience. Others, such as newspaper accounts, reflect the mood of the time as well as the opinions of the papers' editors. All of them give us a unique insight into history as it happened. But it is also important to keep in mind that each source reflects its author's biases, beliefs, and background. Each is still someone's interpretation of an event.

Some of the primary sources in this book will be easy to understand; others may not. Their authors were products of different backgrounds and levels of education. So as you read their words, you will see that some of those words may be spelled differently than we would spell them. And some of their stories may be written without the kinds of punctuation you are used to seeing. Each source has been presented as it was originally written, but wherever a word or phrase is unclear or might be misunderstood, an explanation has been added.

TIME LINE OF WORLD WAR I

1914 —JUNE 28: Archduke Franz Ferdinand of Austria, heir to the Austro-Hungarian throne, is assassinated.

—JULY 28–AUGUST 6: The nations of the Central Powers (Germany and Austria-Hungary) and the Triple Entente (Britain, France, and Russia) declare war on each other. World War I begins.

—AUGUST 4: President Woodrow Wilson declares United States' neutrality in World War I.

—SEPTEMBER 5–10: First Battle of the Marne leads to a stalemate on the western front that will last until the summer of 1918 and cost millions of lives.

1915 —FEBRUARY 4: Germany begins unrestricted submarine warfare.

—MAY 7: A U-boat (German submarine) sinks the passenger liner *Lusitania*, killing 1,198 civilians, including 128 Americans.

—AUGUST 30: Germany responds to American outrage over the *Lusitania* sinking by stopping unrestricted submarine warfare.

1916 —FEBRUARY 21–DECEMBER 18: Battle of Verdun, the longest battle of the war, results in more than one million casualties.

—JULY 1–NOVEMBER 18: Battle of the Somme claims more than one million casualties.

—NOVEMBER 7: President Wilson is reelected for a second term as United States president, using the slogan, "He kept us out of war."

1917 —JANUARY: The secret Zimmermann telegram in which Germany asks Mexico to join it in a war against the neutral United States is discovered and publicized.

—FEBRUARY 1: Germany again declares unrestricted submarine warfare.

—MARCH 15: Catastrophic Russian losses and a people's revolt force Czar Nicholas II of Russia to abdicate, or give up his throne.

—APRIL: Half a million French soldiers "go on strike" and refuse to attack the Germans, but then decide to continue with the war.

—APRIL 2: President Wilson asks Congress for a declaration of war.

—APRIL 6: Congress declares war on Germany.

—MAY: The Creel Committee begins issuing official United States pro-war propaganda.

—MAY 18: Selective Service Act passed by Congress leads to the drafting of 3 million American soldiers (another million enlist voluntarily).

—JUNE: American doughboys begin trickling into France.

—JUNE 15: American Espionage Act is passed. It severely limits freedom of speech and results in nine hundred Americans being jailed for speaking out against the war.

—OCTOBER: The United States suffers its first casualties of the war in the trenches.

—NOVEMBER 7: Bolsheviks (Communists) come to power in Russia.

—DECEMBER: Russia withdraws from the war, allowing many German troops to be moved from the eastern front to the western front.

1918 —JANUARY 8: President Wilson presents his Fourteen Points for a fair peace.

—MARCH–JUNE: Major German offensive launched to try to win the war before too many American troops can reach the western front.

—MAY 28: Americans capture the village of Cantigny, first small victory for American doughboys.

—JUNE 3–4: German advance on Paris is blocked by Americans and French at Chateau-Thierry.

—JUNE 6–26: German advance on Paris is blocked by Americans at Belleau Wood.

—AUGUST 8: "Black Day" for the German Army as the British, French, and Americans break through the German lines and force a major retreat.

—SEPTEMBER 12–16: Doughboys attack the St. Mihiel salient, a bulge in the American line, driving the Germans back and ridding the western front of the bulge.

—SEPTEMBER 26–NOVEMBER 11: Americans fight the brutal Meuse-Argonne campaign, pushing the Germans back slowly through the Argonne Forest, but suffering 120,000 casualties, nearly one tenth of the United States force in France. British and French rapidly push the Germans back along their lines.

—OCTOBER: American troops win battle for the city of Sedan.

—NOVEMBER 9: Battlefield defeats, starvation, and a growing revolt by the German people force Kaiser Wilhelm II of Germany to abdicate.

—NOVEMBER 11: At 11:00 A.M., an armistice brings peace to the western front and ends World War I.

1919 —JANUARY: American troops begin returning home, though many will stay in Europe for much of the year.

—JANUARY–JUNE 28: The Versailles Treaty is written. It blames Germany and punishes it harshly for the war. Many of Wilson's Fourteen Points are ignored. However, the treaty does include a covenant for Wilson's League of Nations.

—AUGUST–SEPTEMBER: Wilson struggles with Congress and tries to convince the American people to ratify the Versailles Treaty and join the League of Nations. He fails, and America again isolates itself from Europe. America's unwillingness to participate weakens the League of Nations, leading to the League's failure and eventually World War II.

—OCTOBER 2: President Wilson suffers a major stroke and is completely disabled for the last six months of his presidency. He dies in 1924, disheartened by his inability to bring peace to the world.

1920 —AUGUST 26: The Nineteenth Amendment, assuring voting rights for women by saying that the right to vote cannot be denied on the basis of sex, is ratified by Congress. Its passage is partly due to the vital war work done by American women.

1939 —SEPTEMBER: Adolf Hitler, an embittered German Army veteran of World War I, orders the invasion of Poland, starting World War II.

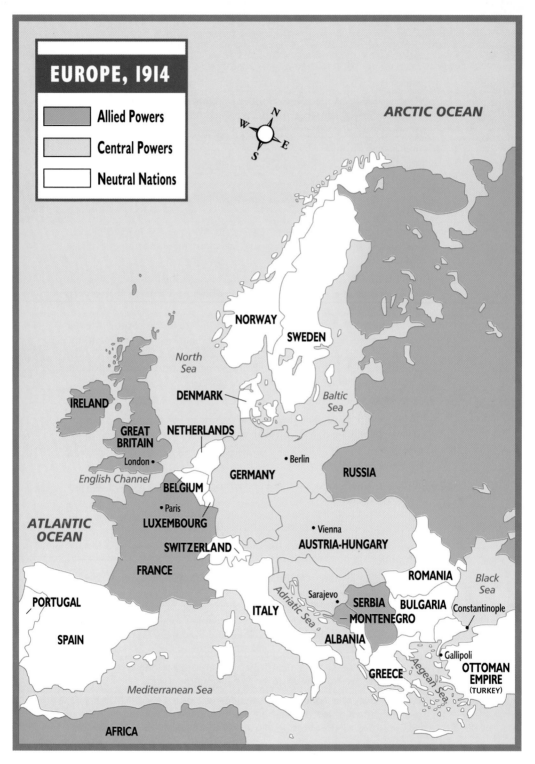

EUROPE, 1914

Allied Powers
Central Powers
Neutral Nations

ARCTIC OCEAN

N
W   E
S

NORWAY
SWEDEN

North
Sea

Baltic
Sea

IRELAND

DENMARK

GREAT
BRITAIN

NETHERLANDS

London •

• Berlin

GERMANY

RUSSIA

English Channel

BELGIUM

• Paris

LUXEMBOURG

ATLANTIC
OCEAN

SWITZERLAND

• Vienna

AUSTRIA-HUNGARY

FRANCE

ROMANIA

Black
Sea

PORTUGAL

Adriatic Sea

Sarajevo
•

SERBIA

BULGARIA

Constantinople

ITALY

MONTENEGRO

•

SPAIN

ALBANIA

GREECE

Aegean Sea

Gallipoli
•

OTTOMAN
EMPIRE
(TURKEY)

Mediterranean Sea

AFRICA

▲ The alignment of Europe at the outbreak of World War I, in 1914. As the war progressed, Italy, Greece, and Portugal were aligned with the Allied Powers, and Bulgaria and Turkey were aligned with the Central Powers.

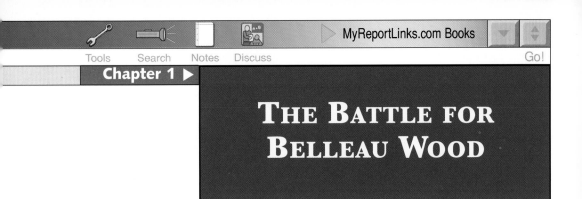

THE BATTLE FOR BELLEAU WOOD

The young, inexperienced American soldiers and Marines who hunched in the trenches facing Belleau Wood, France, on June 6, 1918, had come a long way to fight.

Starting in the spring of 1917, these store clerks, farmers, and factory workers had enlisted or been drafted into the United States armed forces. They had gathered at training camps across America where they learned to march, follow orders, shoot, and plunge a bayonet into sawdust-filled sacks. They then sailed across the Atlantic Ocean, suffered seasickness, and feared U-boat submarine attacks. They landed in France and trained for many more weeks.

Now they were ready to go into battle in a war that had been raging in Europe for nearly four years. That war, World War I, pitted the Germans and Austro-Hungarians against the French, British, and Russians. Later, other countries, including the United States, were drawn into the bloody conflict characterized by trench warfare—fighting between miles of ditches dug into the earth to protect troops from grenades, machine guns, and poison-gas attacks. Even when trenches provided protection

▲ American soldiers wave to those they are leaving behind as they set sail for France—and war—in 1917.

from those weapons, they were places of misery, disease, and death.

▶ The Americans Arrive

In March 1918, the Germans launched a massive attack all along the western front, a continuous battle line of trenches that stretched four hundred miles from the French Alps to the English Channel.

The German soldiers outnumbered the British and French soldiers who faced them across the trenches. The Germans hoped they could crush the British and French armies and win the war quickly before too many Americans reached the battlefield.

Fewer than a million American troops had arrived in France by June 1918, but the United States Army's commanding general, John Pershing,

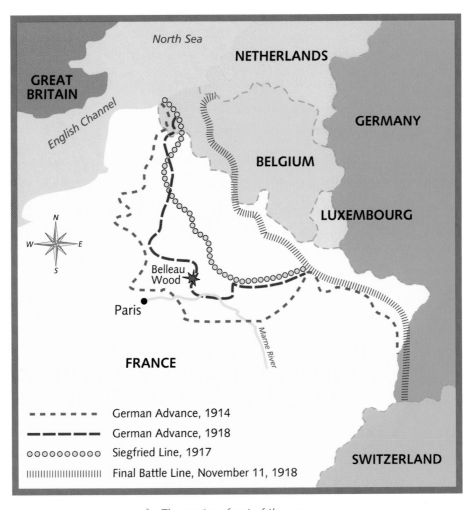

The western front of the war.

was determined that they should help push the Germans back. "I am here for the express purpose of telling you that the Americans will be proud to be engaged in the greatest battle of history," Pershing told the French.[1] He then rushed the young Marines to Belleau Wood to fill a hole in the French line where German troops were pouring through and advancing fast on Paris.

"With only a few hours preparation we were hustled on trucks . . . and tore across country for a whole day. All afternoon our long line of camions [trucks] passed refugees and refugees (hundreds of them—it was pathetic beyond all words)," wrote Lieutenant H. R. Long of Saranac Lake, New York, in a letter that was published in the *Adirondack Express,* a local newspaper. Long told how the French civilians fled the rapidly advancing German Army:

> Farm wagons, baby carriages, wheel barrows, crying kiddies in tired women's arms, old men, resigned and fatalistic sort of looking, laughing girls riding on hay wagons, holding on to cows and horses, women, bird cages and bundles in their arms, bravely trudging along westward. . . .[2]

Arriving at Belleau Wood, the Marines and Army infantry soldiers hurriedly dug shallow body-length trenches with their mess-kit lids and bayonets. "Our graves," they grimly called these little ditches.[3]

When the German attack came against them, the Americans stopped it cold.

Now the troops were ready to begin their counterattack on June 6, 1918, finally "going over the top" for the first time. The Marines waited nervously in the slight safety of their trenches. Then their officers blew shrill whistles and the men leaped out of their holes and charged across no-man's-land—a maze of shell holes and a tangle of barbed wire. They

▲ *American soldiers leaving their trenches, going over the top.*

attacked the German lines as part of the first major United States offensive of World War I. However, for some, this first big attack was the end of the journey.

"Brother 'Billy' and I were of the first 1,250 [soldiers] to go 'over the top.' Eight hundred of these were either killed or wounded, almost before we got started," wrote Joyce Lewis in a letter to a friend after the Battle of Belleau Wood.

I saw Major Berry [wounded], and shortly thereafter "Billy" went down. He was about two hundred feet from me. The boys were charging into machine-gun nests and Billy was running along the edge of a wheat-field toward a wood where Germans were concealed. The first bullet hit him in the top of the head and others lower down as he fell.[4]

Despite the death of his brother and many friends, Joyce Lewis and his comrades rushed across open ground into Belleau Wood, a square mile of hillside covered in scruffy trees, brush, and boulders. The Germans used this rugged terrain to their advantage, digging in, and creating an almost impenetrable fortress. Lewis wrote:

In the charge, I got within fifty feet of the German machine-gun nests when a bullet plowed through the top of my skull. It was a bad wound. . . . As I lay there I could plainly see the German gunners and hear them talking. They could see I was not dead and I watched them as they prepared to finish me. They reloaded

 *German soldiers captured by the Americans at Belleau Wood.*

their gun and turned it on me. The first three bullets went through my legs and hip and the rest splashed up dust and dirt around my head and body. Evidently thinking they had done a good job the Boches [Germans] turned their gun to other parts of the field.[5]

Although Belleau Wood was not strategically important to the Germans, their soldiers fought fiercely to hold it. Though the German Army could have sidestepped around the forest and the Marines to thrust quickly toward Paris, their commander wanted to break the morale of the "green," or inexperienced, American troops. But the Americans proved to be tough fighters.

Joyce Lewis lay wounded in the wheat field, staying utterly still. Playing dead within sight of the German machine guns, he waited hours for help to come.

> That night, about two o'clock, one of my comrades, Robert Hess, of St. Paul, who later in the battle was himself killed, crawled out and started to carry me back to the lines. When he had gone some two hundred feet he stumbled, making a noise such as the Germans heard, and they turned their guns our way. Hess dropt me and, thinking it impossible for him to get me to the lines alone, he piled up a half-dozen bodies of my poor dead "buddies" and barricaded my position. There I remained for several hours longer, and finally during a lull in the battle I was gotten back to the lines. . . . [T]he surgeons came out, finally, and seeing me, exclaimed, "What, ain't you dead yet?" Then they took me into the hospital, fixt me up as best they could, and sent me to Paris in an automobile ambulance.[6]

The rest of the Marines kept fighting in the wood for nearly the whole month of June, capturing, then losing, then recapturing pieces of the tiny forest in desperate hand-to-hand combat. French artillery helped the Americans by mercilessly smashing the German position, wrote Lieutenant Long.

> We gave them 24 hours of 150s and 75s [cannon shells] and then advanced under a rolling [artillery] barrage

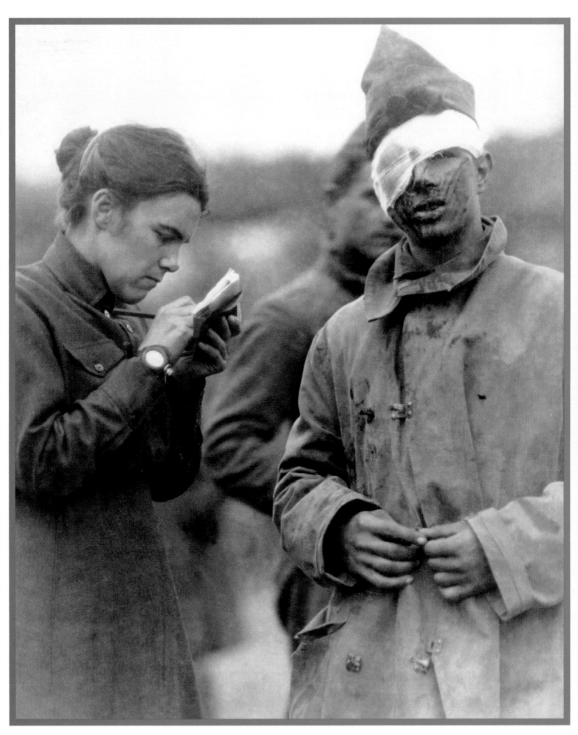

▲ *A Salvation Army worker writes a letter home for a wounded American soldier.*

of 75s. [German machine gun] nests survived this rain of high explosives and shrapnel, but the woods were a wreck. We followed up our barrage all right, but in the progress of the attack the enemy machine guns still held out and we left them to be mopped up later. It was bloody, nasty work. The Marines just threw away their lives—they couldn't be held back.[7]

On June 26, a final charge by the Americans ended the battle for Belleau Wood. The Marines had won, but at the terrible cost of 9,777 men killed or wounded. The French were inspired by the victory and by the end of June 1917 had begun driving the Germans back along the entire battlefront. Some historians say that Belleau Wood, though it was a very small fight in comparison to other World War I battles, marked the beginning of the end for Germany.

The German soldiers, rather than shattering the American will to fight, had instead been impressed by the fighting of the Americans, although they questioned their tactics in fighting in the open and suffering so many losses. A German intelligence report captured at the height of the battle described the Americans' bravery:

The various attacks by both of the Marine regiments were carried out with vigor and regardless of losses. . . . The spirit of the troops is fresh and one of careless confidence. A characteristic expression of one of the [American] prisoners is "we kill or get killed."[8]

Marine Laurence W. Thomsen, who was shot in both legs, wrote home proudly from his hospital bed: "We marched right into the Huns [Germans] and showed them what kind of stuff the marines are made of. They call us 'Devil Dogs'—some distinction."[9]

The Battle of Belleau Wood did not end the war. The growing United States Army and Marine Corps, called the American Expeditionary Force (the AEF), fought many more battles. The AEF helped the French and British push the German Army into retreat throughout 1918, winning big fights at the St. Mihiel salient (a military position that projects into enemy territory), and in the Meuse-Argonne forest.

The quiet scene left behind at Belleau Wood was one of death and destruction. That scene was described by the assistant secretary of the Navy and future American president Franklin D. Roosevelt several weeks after the battle:

In order to enter the wood itself we had to thread our way past water-filled shell holes and thence up the steep slope over outcropping rocks, overturned boulders, down[ed] trees, hastily improvised shelter pits, rusty bayonets, broken guns, emergency ration tins, hand grenades, discarded overcoats, rain-stained love letters, crawling lines of ants and many little mounds [temporary graves], some wholly unmarked, some with a rifle stuck bayonet down in the earth, some with a helmet, and some, too, with a whittled cross with a tag of wood or wrapping paper hung over it and in a pencil scrawl an American name.[10]

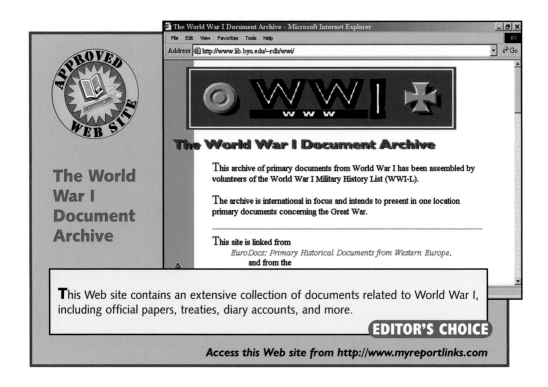

The World War I Document Archive

The World War I Document Archive

This archive of primary documents from World War I has been assembled by volunteers of the World War I Military History List (WWI-L).

The archive is international in focus and intends to present in one location primary documents concerning the Great War.

This site is linked from
EuroDocs: Primary Historical Documents from Western Europe.
and from the

The World War I Document Archive

This Web site contains an extensive collection of documents related to World War I, including official papers, treaties, diary accounts, and more.

EDITOR'S CHOICE

Access this Web site from http://www.myreportlinks.com

French general Jean Degoutte renamed the ravaged forest to thank the Americans for their sacrifice in defense of Paris and his nation. He called it *Bois de la Brigade de Marine*—"the wood of the Marine brigade."[11]

Chapter 2

A BRIEF HISTORY OF WORLD WAR I

Wars have many causes, but there is often a single spark that starts them. For World War I, that spark came on June 28, 1914.

On that day, the heir to the throne of Austria-Hungary, Archduke Franz Ferdinand, and his wife, Sophie, visited the city of Sarajevo in Europe's Balkans, a region "annexed," or taken over, by Austria-Hungary in 1908. Angry Serbian nationalists wanted to free the Balkan people from Austria-Hungary, and

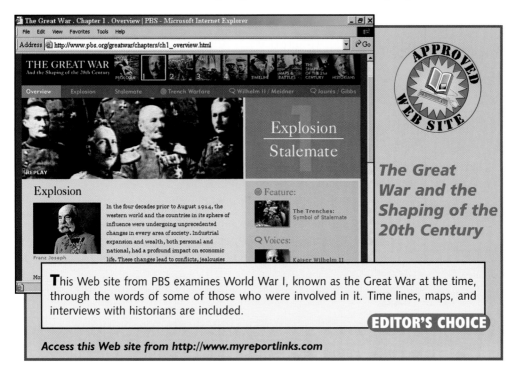

The Great War and the Shaping of the 20th Century

This Web site from PBS examines World War I, known as the Great War at the time, through the words of some of those who were involved in it. Time lines, maps, and interviews with historians are included.

EDITOR'S CHOICE

Access this Web site from http://www.myreportlinks.com

a few thought that terrorism was the best way to advance their cause. Seven of those revolutionaries were waiting for the archduke with bombs and pistols. One of the terrorists, Borijove Jevtic, gave this account of what happened as the archduke's car turned into a Sarajevo street:

Here [Gavrilo] Princip had taken his stand. As the car came abreast he stepped forward from the curb, drew his automatic pistol from his coat and fired two shots. The first struck the wife of the Archduke, the Archduchess Sofia, in the abdomen. She was an expectant mother. . . . The second bullet struck the Archduke close to the heart.[1]

Count Franz von Harrach, who was riding in the archduke's car, reacted with horror:

[A] thin stream of blood spurted from His Highness's [the Archduke's] mouth onto my right cheek. As I was pulling out my handkerchief to wipe the blood away from his mouth, the Duchess cried out to him, "In Heaven's name, what has happened to you?" At that she slid off the seat and lay on the floor of the car, with her face between his knees. . . . Then I heard His Imperial Highness say, "Sopherl, Sopherl, don't die. Stay alive for the children!"[2]

The wounds were fatal. Within minutes, both the archduke and his wife were dead. Soldiers grabbed

Gavrilo Princip, the assassin, and beat him nearly to death. Jevtic tells of Princip's imprisonment:

> Awakened in the middle of the night and told that he was to be carried off to another prison, Princip made an appeal to the prison governor: "There is no need to carry me to another prison. My life is already ebbing away. I suggest that you nail me to a cross and burn me alive. My flaming body will be a torch to light my people on their path to freedom."[3]

Princip died, but his violent deed did not free anyone. Instead, his act triggered World War I, in

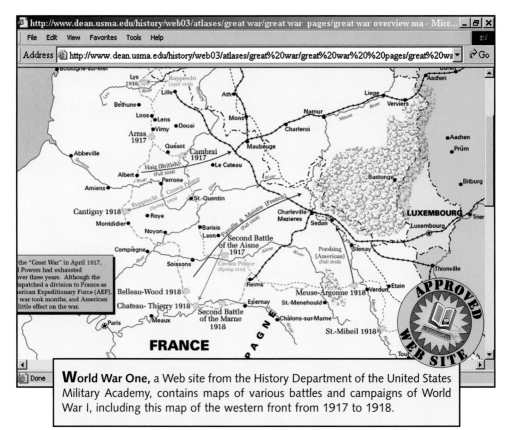

World War One, a Web site from the History Department of the United States Military Academy, contains maps of various battles and campaigns of World War I, including this map of the western front from 1917 to 1918.

which 8.3 million soldiers would be killed and 19.5 million would be wounded, many maimed for life. Included in these terrible casualties were 126,000 American combatants killed and 234,300 wounded.

On the day the archduke died, it is unlikely that any of those doomed Americans could have guessed what lay ahead. At Fourth of July parades held across the country in 1914, "Lining the streets as spectators were men—even boys yet in the grammar grades at school—little suspecting that they were marked even then for foreign service and the soldier's death," wrote John T. Cushing after the war.[4]

The affairs of Europe seemed far away and unimportant to most Americans during that summer of 1914. Young Americans were more interested in the fierce rivalry between the New York Yankees and Cleveland Indians for baseball's American League pennant. Europe endured three years of bloody warfare before the United States was drawn into World War I in 1917.

The Causes of the War

Historians often have a difficult time determining the causes of a war. In the case of World War I, the causes date back to the nineteenth century and a tremendous rivalry between the great European powers. The powerful nations of Great Britain, France, Germany, Italy, Austria-Hungary, and Russia fought each other at times throughout those years. They also competed violently with each other for new colonies in Africa and elsewhere in the world. By 1914, these nations had built up large armies equipped with new weapons, such as machine guns, to threaten their neighbors or defend colonial empires. The European nations also forged secret defense treaties with each other. These secret treaties went into motion when Franz Ferdinand was assassinated.

While the assassinations were the work of a small band of independent Serbian terrorists, Austro-Hungarian diplomats used the murders as an excuse to invade the little nation of Serbia.

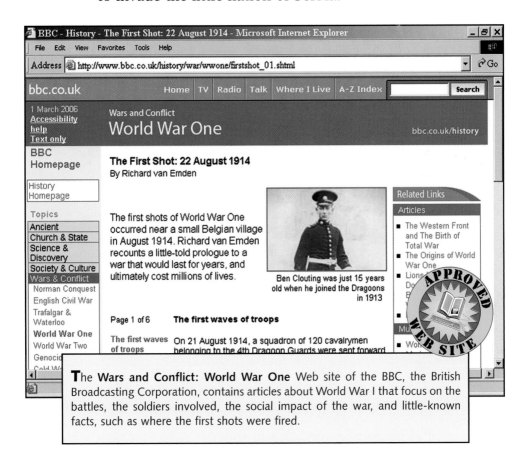

The **Wars and Conflict: World War One** Web site of the BBC, the British Broadcasting Corporation, contains articles about World War I that focus on the battles, the soldiers involved, the social impact of the war, and little-known facts, such as where the first shots were fired.

▶ Alliances Lead to War

On July 28, 1914, Austria-Hungary declared war on Serbia. Two days later, Russia kept its treaty obligation to defend Serbia and declared war on Austria-Hungary. On August 1, Germany, allied with Austria-Hungary, declared war on Russia. France, allied with Russia, then mobilized its troops. On August 3, the Germans, fearing an attack from the French, declared war on France. The next day, the Germans invaded neutral Belgium in a surprise assault. The British kept their defense treaty with Belgium and declared war on Germany.

Within a week, the sides in the Great War, which would later be called World War I, had formed: The Central Powers of Germany and Austria-Hungary, and later, the Ottoman Empire, fought against the Triple Entente of Britain, France, and Russia, later to be joined by Italy and the United States, a group of nations also known as the Allies. So it was that the deaths of two minor members of European royalty led to a disastrous war almost no one wanted.

▶ From Mobilization to the Marne

World War I unleashed four years of some of the worst human slaughter the world has ever witnessed. Unfortunately, Europe's monarchs—King George V of Great Britain, Kaiser Wilhelm II of Germany, Emperor Franz Joseph of Austria-Hungary, and Czar Nicholas II of Russia—had little idea of the horrors to come when they went to war. In the recent past, wars were usually over quickly and casualties were often light, while the amount of territory and prestige that could be claimed by the winners was often huge.

Unfortunately, things had changed dramatically by 1914. Outdated nineteenth-century military tactics such as massed troop formations and cavalry charges on horseback were matched against new twentieth-century technology such as machine guns, airplanes, poison gas, and long-range artillery. The result was a drawn-out bloodbath.

Few people understood the nightmare that lay ahead. American journalist Mildred Aldrich who lived in France in 1914 was one who did understand. She predicted, "It will be the bloodiest affair

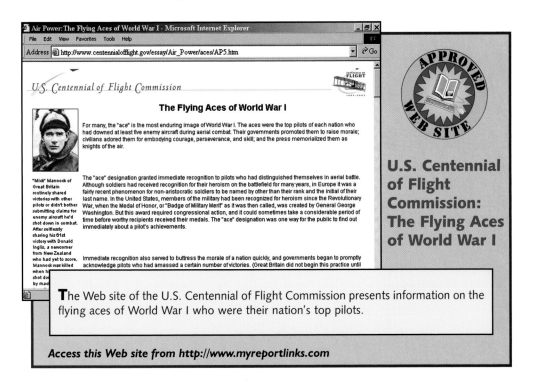

U.S. Centennial of Flight Commission: The Flying Aces of World War I

The Web site of the U.S. Centennial of Flight Commission presents information on the flying aces of World War I who were their nation's top pilots.

Access this Web site from http://www.myreportlinks.com

The National Archives Learning Curve | The Great War | Why did Britain go to war? | Public opin - Micro... _ 🗗 ✕

File   Edit   View   Favorites   Tools   Help

Address 🔲 http://www.learningcurve.gov.uk/greatwar/g2/cs3/g2cs3s3a.htm ▾ ⮎ Go

In this photograph, a group of British men who worked for the Great Western Railway in London, England, at the outbreak of World War I are pictured.

the world has ever seen—a war in the air, a war under the sea as well as on it, and carried out with the most effective man-slaughtering machines ever used in battle."[5]

The men going off to fight had little idea of what to expect. Many imagined that the war would be a glorious adventure. All over Europe, they put on uniforms and marched off to battle, singing patriotic songs and cheered by flag-waving crowds. Every country assumed it would win a speedy victory. French commandant A. Grasset recalled, "Cries of *'Vive la France! Viva l'armee'* ['Hooray for France!

Hooray for the army!'] could be heard . . . while people waved handkerchiefs and hats. The women were throwing kisses and heaped flowers upon our convoy."[6]

In August 1914, the Germans sent more than a million men charging through neutral Belgium, whose tiny army fought bravely but without success. It was here that the brutality of World War I began. "Towns were sacked and burned, homes were pillaged. . . . Men, women and children, were massed in public squares and mowed down by mitrailleuses [German machine guns]," wrote Brand Whitlock,

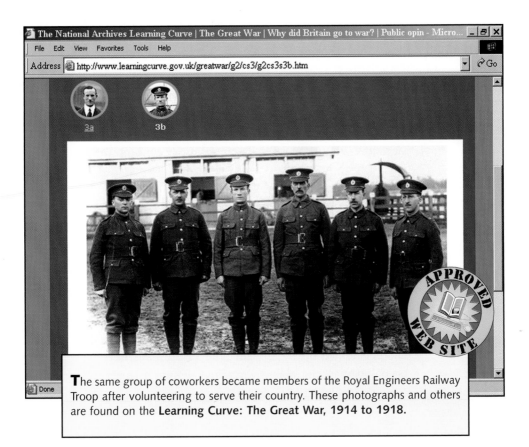

The same group of coworkers became members of the Royal Engineers Railway Troop after volunteering to serve their country. These photographs and others are found on the **Learning Curve: The Great War, 1914 to 1918.**

the United States ambassador to Belgium.[7] These
real atrocities were magnified by false rumors
and propaganda, the spreading of ideas, facts, and
allegations to further one's cause or harm an opponent's. German soldiers, insultingly called "huns,"
"boche," or "fritz," were cast in the most negative
light. Rumors circulated about their viciousness,
saying the Germans bayoneted babies or chopped
off children's hands. This propaganda was used to
whip up British and French patriotism and eventually turn America against Germany.

The Germans had their own version of what
happened in Belgium. In August 1914, German soldier Otto Luening wrote to a relative living in the
United States:

From what I hear here, most of America is against
Germany on account of Belgium. . . . According to
what I have heard, the French & English are cabling
big lies to America in regard to the war. . . . Now I
will tell you some of the appetizing things Belgers
[Belgians] did to the Germans. All of this is true & I
would swear to it. . . . The civilians shoot the soldiers
from behind while they are marching thru villages.
One soldier was shot in the leg. . . . He dropped & the
mob grabbed a hold of him & sawed off both of his
legs with an ordinary saw while he was living!!! One
soldier was found with his eyes cut out! One with his
hands chopped off by an axe! . . . 150 Germans have
been killed in the above ways in Belgium & this is
what they call civilization."[8]

The German Army roared from Belgium into France, toward Paris. American Mildred Aldrich watched the invasion.

[B]etween me and the terrible [battle] stretched a beautiful country, as calm in the sunshine as if horrors were not. It was just about six o'clock when the first bomb that we could really see came over the hill. . . . For two hours we saw them rise, descend, explode. Then a little smoke would rise from one hamlet, then from another; then a tiny flame—hardly more than a spark—would be visible; and by dark the whole plain was on fire.[9]

The French rallied. Using every vehicle they could find, they rushed their army to the front and stopped the German assault. Paris's taxicabs were even pressed into service, delivering reserve troops to the front and saving France's Sixth Army from defeat. Next came the race to the sea as the Germans and the French with their British allies tried to out-flank each other. Neither side could get around the other, and the result was a four-hundred-mile battle line of defensive trenches winding from Switzerland to the English Channel. Meanwhile, the Germans and Austro-Hungarians were fighting the Russians fiercely on the eastern front.

▶ Stalemate

Instead of the quick victory many people expected, the war became a stalemate. From 1915 to 1917, the generals attacked each other between the trenches. The first Battle of Ypres, in Belgium, was followed by the second and then the third. The terrible battles of Verdun and the Somme were followed by many others. Everywhere along the western front, the story at the end of each battle was the same. Millions of young men were sacrificed to gain a few yards of no-man's-land—a moonlike landscape of shell holes, mud, debris, and dead bodies. Then a short time later, the other side would take back that same piece of scarred landscape at a terrible cost in men killed and wounded.

Strangely, the generals never learned that frontal attacks against machine guns were suicidal. They continued to hope for a breakthrough with each new attack. "I feel that every step in my plan has been taken with the Divine help,"[10] wrote British general Douglas Haig about his attack at the Battle of the Somme on July 1, 1916. Haig's plan was just another disaster. The British 8th Division began the battle that day with 8,500 troops. Two hours into the attack, charges across no-man's-land had cost the 8th Division 5,492 men.[11] The British Army gained barely a few hundred yards of territory.

"Hell Cannot Be So Terrible"

You can try to imagine how horrible the losses were for the British 8th Division that day by picturing every boy in your school running at full speed down the length of a football field. Then imagine that only

▲ *French soldiers wait in a trench, in the terrifying moments before zero hour—when they will go over the top and into no-man's-land.*

a third of the boys reach the end zone unhurt. The other two thirds are shot or blown up by shells, some dying and others horribly wounded. Then imagine that the next day, more of the boys are lost when the enemy pushes them back to the other end of the field. This goes on day after day, month after month. The casualties during World War I were staggering.

"Humanity . . . must be mad to do what it is doing," wrote a young French lieutenant in his diary during World War I. "What scenes of horror and carnage! . . . Hell cannot be so terrible."[12]

▷ A World at War

The deadlock on the western front forced the combatants to try to find other battlefronts on which to win the war. This led to fighting in Africa and the Middle East and to war on the high seas. The Great War truly became a world war.

No one, not even people from neutral countries, was safe. German submarines known as U-boats (from the German *Unterseeboot,* literally "undersea boat"), sank any nation's ships that were suspected of carrying supplies to Great Britain. This policy of unrestricted submarine warfare caused great hardship in the form of severe food shortages for the British people.

In the spring of 1917, the Russians were crushed by the Germans on the eastern front. Then the Russian people rose up and overthrew Czar Nicholas. That November, the Bolshevik Revolution brought Vladimir Lenin to power, creating a Socialist state. In December, the Communists pulled Russia out of the war, freeing thousands of German soldiers to fight on the western front.

▶ The Sinking of the *Lusitania*

The first Americans to die in World War I were not soldiers. They were innocent passengers on an ocean liner sailing from New York to England. In February 1915, the Germans announced their policy of unrestricted submarine warfare, threatening any ship sailing in British waters. The Germans were especially intent on stopping shiploads of supplies from the United States to help Great Britain's war effort. On May 7, 1915, a German submarine, the U-20, sank the ocean liner *Lusitania*—a ship that

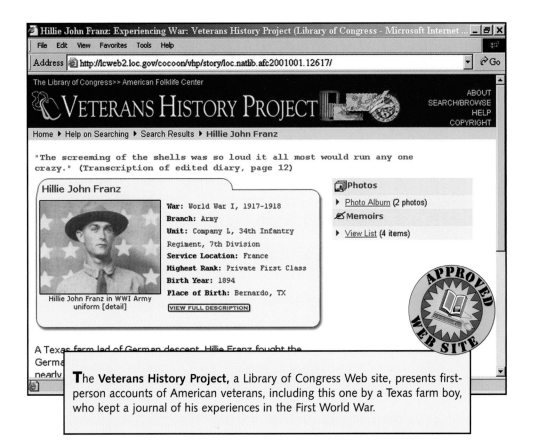

Hillie John Franz: Experiencing War: Veterans History Project (Library of Congress - Microsoft Internet ...

File Edit View Favorites Tools Help

Address http://lcweb2.loc.gov/cocoon/vhp/story/loc.natlib.afc2001001.12617/ Go

The Library of Congress>> American Folklife Center

VETERANS HISTORY PROJECT

ABOUT
SEARCH/BROWSE
HELP
COPYRIGHT

Home ▸ Help on Searching ▸ Search Results ▸ Hillie John Franz

"The screeming of the shells was so loud it all most would run any one crazy." (Transcription of edited diary, page 12)

Hillie John Franz

Hillie John Franz in WWI Army uniform [detail]

War: World War I, 1917-1918
Branch: Army
Unit: Company L, 34th Infantry Regiment, 7th Division
Service Location: France
Highest Rank: Private First Class
Birth Year: 1894
Place of Birth: Bernardo, TX

VIEW FULL DESCRIPTION

Photos
▸ Photo Album (2 photos)
Memoirs
▸ View List (4 items)

APPROVED WEB SITE

A Texas farm lad of German descent, Hillie Franz fought the Germa... nearly...

The Veterans History Project, a Library of Congress Web site, presents first-person accounts of American veterans, including this one by a Texas farm boy, who kept a journal of his experiences in the First World War.

was carrying ammunition to the British. American survivor Charles Jeffery remembered the sinking:

There was a thunderous roar, as of the collapse of a great building on fire. Then the Lusitania disappeared, dragging hundreds of fellow creatures into the vortex. Many never rose to the surface, but the sea rapidly grew black with the figures of struggling men, women and children. [13]

The sinking of the *Lusitania* killed 1,198 people, including 128 Americans, and nearly brought

America into the war against the Germans. Germany then promised to stop unrestricted submarine warfare. Most Americans wanted to stay out of Europe's war, and so did President Woodrow Wilson. In 1916, Wilson ran for reelection with the slogan "He Kept Us Out of War," although it was a slogan he himself never liked, perhaps because the United States was making some preparations for war in 1916. In January 1917, the Germans broke their promise and resumed unrestricted submarine warfare again, making it difficult for the United States to stay out of the war.

▶ The Zimmermann Telegram

Another event in the beginning of 1917 made it even more difficult for the United States to remain neutral. In January, British intelligence intercepted a telegram sent by Arthur Zimmermann, the German foreign minister to the United States, to Heinrich von Eckhardt, Germany's minister to Mexico. In the telegram, Germany promised to give Mexico part of the United States if Mexico would side with Germany and join in an attack on the United States. The telegram was intercepted by the British, and their cryptographers, or code breakers, deciphered it. The British government did not alert President Woodrow Wilson until February 24, in part to protect their own people involved in intelligence gathering and to capitalize on growing anti-German sentiment in the United States. When it was

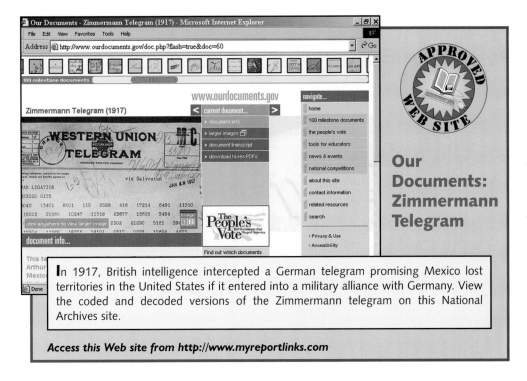

Our Documents: Zimmermann Telegram

In 1917, British intelligence intercepted a German telegram promising Mexico lost territories in the United States if it entered into a military alliance with Germany. View the coded and decoded versions of the Zimmermann telegram on this National Archives site.

Access this Web site from http://www.myreportlinks.com

published in American newspapers on March 1, the Zimmermann telegram had a huge effect on American public opinion. Then in March, two American ships were torpedoed by U-boats.

War fever seized the country. Former president Theodore Roosevelt shouted, "There is no question about going to war. Germany is already at war with us."[14] Anti-German parades displayed banners with the messages "Kill the Kaiser!" or "Let's Get the Hun."[15]

Faced with continuing German threats and attacks, President Wilson asked Congress to declare war on Germany on April 2, 1917. Wilson's speech received a resounding applause, but his public words were followed by personal fears. "Think of what it was they

This patriotic poster of Uncle Sam, symbolizing the United States, was created by James Montgomery Flagg in 1916. More than 4 million copies were printed between 1917 and 1918 as Americans entered World War I.

were applauding," the president told his secretary after the speech. "My message of today was a message of death for our young men. How strange it seems to applaud that."[16] The United States declared war on Germany on April 6, 1917.

But not all Americans were in favor of going to war, and many Americans protested it. As a result, Congress passed the Espionage Act, which empowered the federal government to imprison and silence those who spoke out against the war.

Though President Wilson asked for a million soldiers, only seventy-three thousand volunteered in the first six weeks of the war. Congress passed the Selective Service Act, making it mandatory that men between twenty-one and thirty-one years of age register for the draft. A lottery determined which of those men would have to go to war.

The first American soldiers arrived in France in June 1917, but only a few saw combat by October. It was not until the spring of 1918 that American soldiers began fighting on the western front in large numbers. Once there, those fresh troops from the United States helped break the stalemate and turn the tide against the Germans, bringing the war to an end on November 11, 1918.

▶ Making the World Safe for Democracy

In the words of President Woodrow Wilson, the war had been waged to make the world "safe for democracy," and prevent all future wars. Now that it was over, Wilson worked to come up with a plan for lasting peace.

▲ Woodrow Wilson, center, with the members of the American Commission to Negotiate Peace, Paris, France, 1919.

Wilson's idealistic peace plan, called the Fourteen Points, called for the establishment of an international body known as the League of Nations. Its goal was to prevent future wars among the world's most powerful nations.

Unfortunately, Britain, France, and Italy were not interested in Wilson's idealism. The peace treaty negotiated at Versailles, France, blamed the Germans solely for the war and required Germany to make reparations, or huge payments, to the European countries it had invaded. The Austro-Hungarian Empire was dissolved. Though the Europeans agreed to establish the League of Nations, Wilson was heartbroken when the United States Senate failed to ratify the treaty that established it. By 1919, Americans

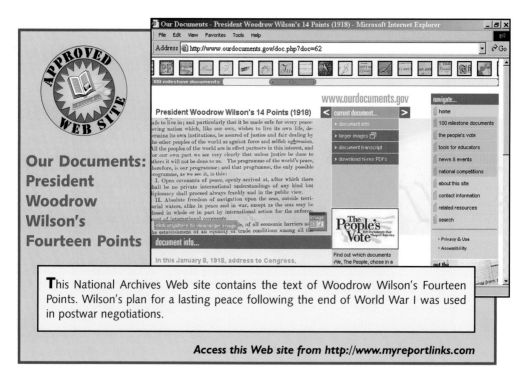

Our Documents: President Woodrow Wilson's Fourteen Points

This National Archives Web site contains the text of Woodrow Wilson's Fourteen Points. Wilson's plan for a lasting peace following the end of World War I was used in postwar negotiations.

Access this Web site from http://www.myreportlinks.com

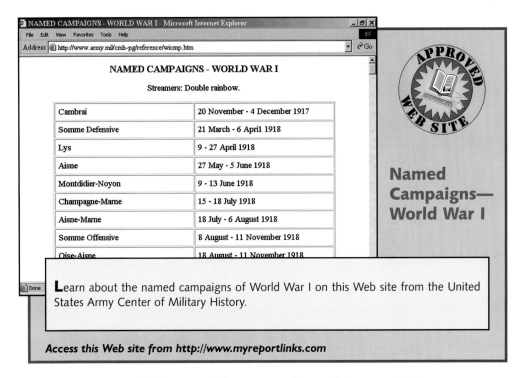

NAMED CAMPAIGNS - WORLD WAR I - Microsoft Internet Explorer

File Edit View Favorites Tools Help

Address http://www.army.mil/cmh-pg/reference/wicmp.htm

NAMED CAMPAIGNS - WORLD WAR I

Streamers: Double rainbow.

Cambrai	20 November - 4 December 1917
Somme Defensive	21 March - 6 April 1918
Lys	9 - 27 April 1918
Aisne	27 May - 5 June 1918
Montdidier-Noyon	9 - 13 June 1918
Champagne-Marne	15 - 18 July 1918
Aisne-Marne	18 July - 6 August 1918
Somme Offensive	8 August - 11 November 1918
Oise-Aisne	18 August - 11 November 1918

Done

Named Campaigns— World War I

Learn about the named campaigns of World War I on this Web site from the United States Army Center of Military History.

Access this Web site from http://www.myreportlinks.com

were fed up with Europe's problems. Without America, the League of Nations was weaker and less able to stop future wars or prevent Germany and other nations from rearming.

The British novelist and pro-war propagandist H. G. Wells called World War I "the war that will end war."[17] He imagined that the sacrifice of the millions who died would lead to a world forever at peace. Many soldiers accepted that belief. "One's revulsion to the ghastly horrors of war was submerged [during the fighting] in the belief that this war was to end all wars and Utopia would arise," remembered Corporal J. H. Tansley, a British Army veteran.[18] Instead, World War I was a ghastly introduction to the bloodiest century of warfare in history.

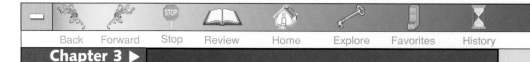
SOLDIERS' STORIES

The United States was unprepared for war in the spring of 1917. The nation had just two hundred thousand men in its army and needed to send 4 million soldiers to France. The army's weapons were old, some dating to 1898, the year of the Spanish-American War. The United States had only a few airplanes and a handful of pilots.

▶ A Call to Arms

After Congress declared war, America rushed to build up its military. Between April and August 1917, sixteen giant training camps were built in various parts of the country to train troops. One recruit, Rex H. Thurston, described his arrival at a camp in Texas, where not a minute was lost in preparing him for war:

Company E, 102nd Infantry Regiment, United States Army. This Connecticut unit fought at Chateau Thierry, St. Mihiel, and the Meuse-Argonne.

When we got off the train which stopped right in the camp, we were chased up to a barracks where we were examined for contagious diseases. . . . We were then passed into a room where we stripped and wrapped our clothes in a paper. Our names were taken and placed on the packages. These are sent home by the government. From then on it was all action. We passed through a shower bath and then went in single file to doctor after doctor. . . . Our finger prints were taken, all scars recorded and they began to hand out clothes. . . . [and then we] marched out the front door dressed like soldiers but feeling a long way from being one.[1]

At first, the recruits found themselves training with wooden guns and artillery rather than the real things, which were in short supply. Still, the training was difficult. One recruit sent a postcard home telling of the tough schedule endured by new soldiers:

From 7:30 to 10:45 we have infantry drill, bayonet drill and physical exercise. That doesn't mean 5 minutes drill and rest either . . . A total 20 minutes rest in that time. We generally have . . . combat problems

between 1:00 and 4:00 pm rain, mud or dust. . . .
[Then] a hike of several miles. . . .[2]

The newly trained American soldiers were nick-named doughboys. Some suggest the name comes from the doughy flour dumplings that American soldiers roasted at the ends of their bayonets. Other think it may have originated with the large buttons on soldiers' uniforms that looked like dough balls.[3] Whatever its origin, the name caught on as America's young men went off to fight.

Once trained, the doughboys were rushed by railroad to ports in the United States and shipped to France. For many, it was the first time they had left their hometowns, and the trip was exciting. Private Joseph Reisacker described the experience in a letter:

Well Minnie I never had a better time in my life than I did on this trip. . . . When we went through a city we were all hanging out the windows and yelling with all our might [W]e were met at every station by people [T]hey were sure glad to see us [T]hey waved flags and thrower [threw] kisses at us [A]t home the people are nothing like the people here [T]hey are more con-nected with the war. . . . [T]ell everybody that I am on my way and am going to keep going till I get to Berlin [the German capital].[4]

At first, the journey to France was exciting too, but it soon became boring because the soldiers had little to do on board ship. Seasickness was a problem for farm boys and city slickers alike, since many had never seen, let alone been on, an ocean before. As Sergeant Edwin Gerth wrote in his diary, "On July 15th, we started our voyage, at 7 am, on the transport [ship] Northern Pacific. The first day was quite thrilling with the destroyers dashing around us and a dirigible balloon and seaplane above. But the second day—wow ! Sick isn't a strong enough word. . . . I got sick whenever I went below [deck]."[5]

▶ On the Alert

The ship convoys kept a constant watch for U-boats. If observers spotted a submarine, they sounded the alarm, and Navy destroyers went into action. The destroyers laid down smoke screens to hide the troopships from enemy submarines and dropped depth charges meant to sink the U-boats. These exploded and sent huge columns of water into the air. Most U-boat "attacks" turned out to be false alarms, like the following described by Private Otis E. Briggs: "At 1:15 PM the alarm bells sounded while we were attending a lecture. We hurried . . . as the guns boomed . . . on deck. The sub was a porpoise."[6]

The Navy convoys did a great job of getting back and forth across the Atlantic Ocean. Few ships were sunk, but S. J. Premo was an eyewitness to one successful U-boat attack.

We left Liverpool [England] with three other passenger boats protected by a convoy of destroyers. When we had been under way three days . . . the alarm sounded, telling us that periscopes had been sighted. . . . We dropped a number of depth bombs, or "ash cans", as they were called . . . and hoped for the best. The destroyers rushed around like mad, seeking periscopes to shoot at. I stood at the rail, looking at the "Cedric", one of our sister ships about half a mile away, when a column of white water suddenly shot up near her bow. In a few seconds I heard a dull boom, not very loud, but giving the impression of terrific force let loose. A second torpedo struck. . . . Six hundred [men], if I remember, were lost on the "Cedric."[7]

▷ "Lafayette—We Are Here!"

The first American troops to arrive in France got there just in time. The arrival of the Americans boosted the spirits of the French and helped make France's soldiers want to finish the war. On July 4, 1917, Parisians celebrated the arrival of the troops of the American Expeditionary Force. Private Otis E. Briggs recalls the excitement:

Everyone is gathering along the streets to witness the parade, all dressed in their best. The parade starts, led by a representative detail of English and French troops. Next comes several thousand negro stevedores [U.S. army dockworkers] and then the Engineers followed by ambulances. . . . "Vive L'Amerique! Vive L'Amerique!" is shouted. The applause increases. We approach the reviewing stand. "Eyes Right!" We are passing [U.S.] General [John] Pershing who stands at ease watching with a critical eye.[8]

 *General Pershing offers a salute at Lafayette's tomb.*

A ceremony that day at Lafayette's tomb caught the world's attention. The Marquis de Lafayette had come to the aid of the Continental Army in 1777, serving bravely during the American war for independence, the Revolutionary War. AEF colonel Charles E. Stanton acknowledged America's debt:

The fact cannot be forgotten that your nation [France] was our friend when America was struggling for existence . . . that France in the person of Lafayette came to our aid in words and deed. . . . Therefore it is with loving pride . . . in the shadow of the illustrious dead we [the American soldiers] pledge our hearts and our honor in carrying this war to successful issue. Lafayette—We are here!"[9]

As the days passed, doughboys by the thousands poured into France. As Private Hazen S. Helmrich pointed out, their arrival was often dampened by the realities of war:

We gathered by the rail [of the ship] and gazed for the first time at the brilliantly lighted harbor and realized that we were in France. . . . While we were waiting on deck with our full equipment on, a trainload of 500 wounded came in on the wharf beside us. They were brought on board at once. About half of them were suffering from gas poisoning. [Poison gas was a weapon used by both sides in the war]. Their skin was yellow and their eyes were protected from the sun by paper shades. Many had both legs amputated.[10]

Private Allan Neil in a letter home told of the sad scenes that greeted him as he moved across France toward the battlefield:

Mother—There are so many women [in France] wearing black and the other [women] show what a strain they have been thru. There are scarcely any young [French]men seen except those who have returned minus some part of their anatomy or else in such a physical condition that they are almost helpless. All

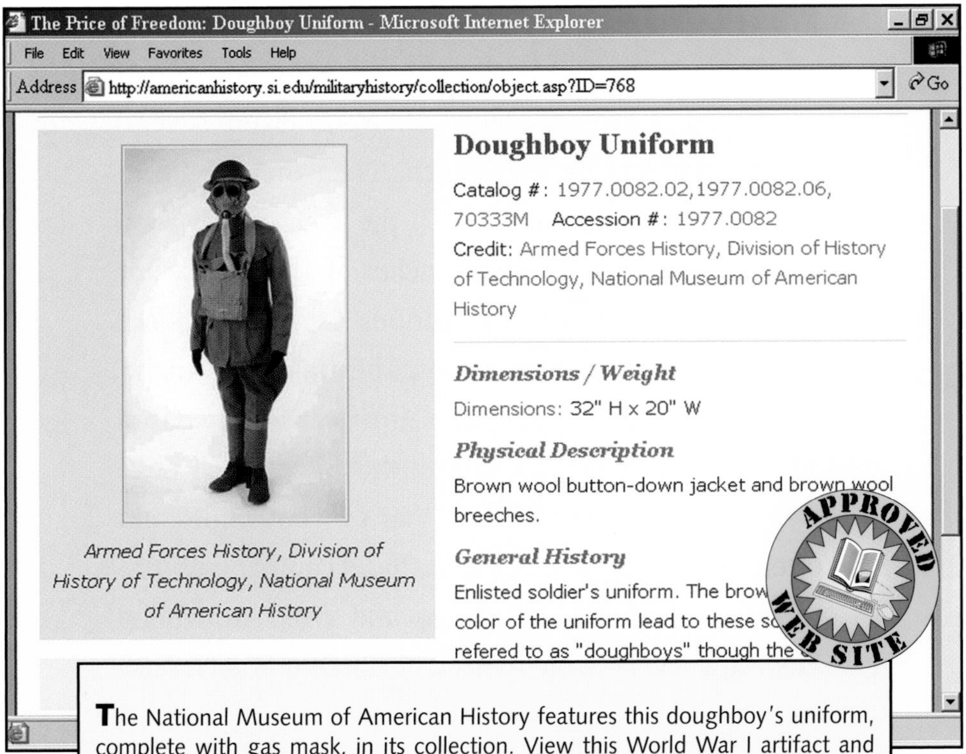
The Price of Freedom: Doughboy Uniform - Microsoft Internet Explorer
File Edit View Favorites Tools Help
Address http://americanhistory.si.edu/militaryhistory/collection/object.asp?ID=768
Go
Doughboy Uniform
Catalog #: 1977.0082.02,1977.0082.06, 70333M Accession #: 1977.0082
Credit: Armed Forces History, Division of History of Technology, National Museum of American History
Dimensions / Weight
Dimensions: 32" H x 20" W
Physical Description
Brown wool button-down jacket and brown wool breeches.
General History
Enlisted soldier's uniform. The brow
color of the uniform lead to these so
refered to as "doughboys" though the
Armed Forces History, Division of History of Technology, National Museum of American History
APPROVED WEB SITE

The National Museum of American History features this doughboy's uniform, complete with gas mask, in its collection. View this World War I artifact and others at **The Price of Freedom: Americans at War,** a Smithsonian Web site.

EDITOR'S CHOICE

> the men working are over fifty and then there are lots of boys. . . .[11]

By the time the United States Army had reached its peak size, on November 11, 1918, it numbered 3,703,273 soldiers, with 2,003,935 of them actually reaching France. The army in France was mostly white, but it also included 13,000 American Indians, plus 200,000 black Americans. Of those African Americans, about 158,000 were in noncombat units and 42,000 served in combat units, but all were segregated.

▷ Trench Warfare

The inexperienced American troops were not rushed to the front immediately but were given several months training by the French. Then they began to see combat. In October 1917, the U.S. 1st Division took up its position in the trenches of a "quiet" sector on the western front. The curious Germans did not leave the sector quiet for long. They launched night-time trench raids against the Americans and caused the first American casualties of the war. Trench raids were used throughout World War I by both sides and often resulted in fierce hand-to-hand combat with pistols, bayonets, knives, clubs, and fists. Doughboy Edward Luckert wrote to his wife about one such raid:

[L]ast night we went out as usual, crawling thru the Boche wire. . . . we suspected that Fritz [the Germans] might lay in wait to ambush us. . . . [Suddenly] we heard a smothered cough directly in front of us. And then the ground seemed to spring up in one great roar and flame and we knew it had been a trap. . . . [T]he only thing to do was back out the way we came in. . . . All this time they continued to pepper us with grenades and pistols. . . . Once again within our own [barbed] wire—the firing stopped and I took account of losses. A'Hearn was hit five times all around his hips and thighs. Lt. Brown had his face looking like a piece of beef and four of the men including Williams had been hit in the chest and limbs. . . . Then for the first time I looked at my watch. Only a half hour [had passed] since we went out until we got back![12]

 *German soldiers in the Argonne, a wooded region in northeastern France between the Meuse and Aisne rivers where Americans fought.*

As 1917 dragged into 1918, more Americans poured into the trenches and joined in battles that grew larger. Americans played the leading roles in victories at Cantigny, Chateau-Thierry, Belleau Wood, the St. Mihiel salient, and in the Meuse-Argonne campaign. While General Pershing kept track of over-all strategy, the war in the trenches often looked like total confusion to the soldiers, and their day-to-day lives there were miserable, as Private William Bishop, Jr., reported in this letter home:

Pleasure around here there isn't much except reading your shirt, which means to look it over for cooties

[lice]. An[d] as for rats, they are the size of a five-year old tom cat. You can't scare them. They crawl all over your bunks, and if you knock them down they just come right back again. If the Boche [Germans] had as much nerve as the rats or trench rabbits as we call them, we certainly would have a time of it.[13]

The men held their posts no matter what the weather, something Corporal Albert Smith complained about.

This is the wettest muddiest country I ever saw, it has been raining steadily for seven weeks. I stepped in a mud hole the other night and went up to my waist in mud and didnt get to change clothes and in fact I haven't changed yet. I haven't changed for over two month and havent even had my clothes off for that length of time. I have not had a bath for six weeks and none in sight. . . . [14]

The daily discomfort of trench warfare could be shattered at any moment by a gas attack. Those who did not put on gas masks fast enough were blinded or strangled to death. So terrible was this weapon that after the war, the world's nations agreed to ban its use. Doughboy Stull Holt wrote home about a gas attack he survived.

[G]as shells started to come in great numbers. . . . I was about buried by a shell and a few seconds later a big gas shell went off within 20 ft of me. Something hit me on the head, making a big dent in my helmet and

Dear Home: Letters From WWI - Microsoft Internet Explorer

File   Edit   View   Favorites   Tools   Help

Address http://www.historychannel.com/letters/stull_holt.html

Letters from WWI • Letter Preservation • Legacy Project • World War I Videos • Veterans Forum • Letter Archive

Dear Home
LETTERS FROM WWI

Letter from Stull Holt

Sept. 1, 1917

Dear Lois,
At last the long delayed and promised letter. You mustn't complain tho because I wrote to no one. All I did when I had a chance to rest was to throw myself in bed, dead to the world. I am in Paris now on permission, a month late, and am enjoying the luxuries of life including ice cream, sheets, cafes and things. What I have done and am doing here I will tell you in a few days, at present I'll only say your last letter (Aug. 13) speaking of my trip to Paris came a day too late.

Nov

Stull Holt writes home about being knocked down by a shell and becoming intoxicated by poisonous gas.

Click here to see actual letter.
▶▶▶

Other Letters
Albert Smith

Edward Lukert

John Douglas

Dear Home: Letters From WWI, a Web site of the History Channel, contains a collection of letters from six soldiers and a nurse who served in World War I, including this one from doughboy Stull Holt.

EDITOR'S CHOICE

raising a bump on my head. If it hadn't been for my helmet my head would have been cracked. As it was I was dazed, knocked down and my gas mask knocked off. I got several breathes of the strong [poison gas] solution right from the shell before it got diluted with much air. If it hadn't been for the fellow with me I probably wouldn't be writing this letter because I couldn't see, my eyes were running water and burning, so was my nose and I could hardly breathe. . . .[15]

The greatest danger faced by the doughboys came in daytime frontal assaults. When Americans "went over the top" of their trenches and charged across no-man's-land, they were easy targets for German machine guns. Private Clifton R. Fields of Arkansas, who served in Company D, 128th Infantry Regiment, 32nd Division, remembered such an attack at the Meuse-Argonne:

On October 15th, 1918, we were charging machine guns and men were being cut down like grass all around me. Then I was hit and fell, and couldn't get up. I laid there on the battlefield for three days and was assumed dead. Some man came by and said: Fields, what the hell are you doing laying there? The man picked . . . [me up and carried me] three miles to the aid station. Gangrene [infection] had already set-up, and they amputated my leg just below the knee. I was passing in and out of consciousness during the whole time and never recognized the man that carried me to safety. . . . I've always regretted never knowing the man that saved my life.[16]

As the war progressed, the Americans won a reputation as tough fighters. Lieutenant Kurt Hesse of the German 5th Grenadiers was stunned by the doughboys' ferocity:

I have never seen so many dead. I have never seen such a frightful spectacle of war. On the other bank [of the river] the Americans, in close combat, had destroyed two of our [German] companies. Lying down in the wheat, [the Americans] had allowed our troops to approach and then annihilated them at a range of 30 to 50 yards. "The Americans kill everyone,"

was the cry of fear . . . a cry that caused our men to tremble for a long time.[17]

Some of the hardest-fighting American troops were those in segregated black infantry units that were part of the final push to victory in autumn 1918. The 369th Infantry Regiment, nicknamed the

▲ An African-American unit of U.S. Army infantrymen marches northwest of Verdun, in northeastern France, during the war.

Harlem Hellfighters, served in the trenches 191 days—longer than any other U.S. unit—and was the first Allied regiment to break through the German lines and reach the Rhine River. One African-American soldier, Andrew Johnson, told of his experiences:

> We were in the [Argonne] Forest when the [b]ig push started on September 26, 1918 and we stayed in there five days, part of the time we were shelled by our own artillery [by accident]. . . . [O]ur . . . runners were all killed or wounded trying to get through with messages. . . . Enemy airplanes flow [flew] over us several times,

▲ Crosses circling the hillside of the Aisne-Marne American cemetery in Belleau, France, mark the graves of Americans killed in the region's battles.

dropping pamphlets addressed to us. [The pamphlets read:] 'Colored Americans. We have no quarrel with you. We are your friends. Throw down your arms and cover [come] over to our side. We will treat you better than you are treated in the [American] South.' But I don't remember a single case of desertion.[18]

By November 1918, the British, French, and Americans had shattered the German lines all along the western front, and the battered German Army was in full retreat. The British naval blockade of Germany had resulted in many German civilians at home starving and had cut Germany's war supplies to almost nothing. The German people rioted in the streets, Kaiser Wilhelm gave up his throne, and Germany asked for peace. At 11 A.M. on November 11, 1918, the Germans signed an armistice, bringing the fighting to an end.

Shortly afterward, an American lieutenant, Lewis Plush, summed up the war in the trenches: "Men fought to kill, to maim, to destroy. Some return home, others remain behind forever on the fields of their greatest sacrifice. There was a war, a great war, and now it is over."[19]

Lewis Plush was one of the lucky ones. He and millions of other Americans returned home to peacetime lives. Back in California, Plush got married, planted apples, and raised turkeys on his ranch. Unfortunately there were 126,000 young Americans who never saw home or their families again.

ABOVE THE LINES, BEHIND THE LINES, AND AFTER THE WAR

The doughboys in the trenches relied on many kinds of support. They needed Allied airplanes to protect them from the German Air Force. They needed equipment and food, tons of which had to be shipped from America to France. They needed nurses and doctors to treat their wounded.

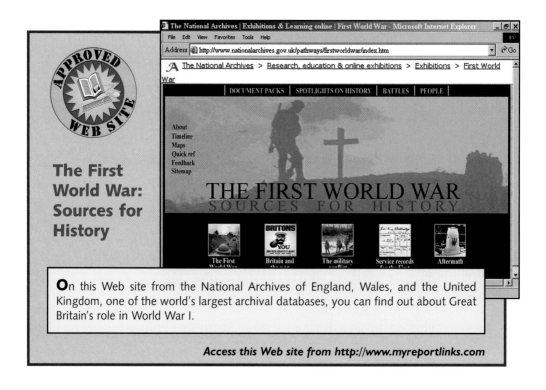

The First World War: Sources for History

On this Web site from the National Archives of England, Wales, and the United Kingdom, one of the world's largest archival databases, you can find out about Great Britain's role in World War I.

Access this Web site from http://www.myreportlinks.com

The War in the Air

The first powered, steerable airplane was built in 1903 by the Wright brothers. Aircraft were used for peaceful purposes until 1914. With the outbreak of World War I, it did not take long to find a way to adapt powered aircraft as a weapon. Tiny fragile fighter planes armed with machine guns fought each other and protected observation balloons used to spy on enemy troops. Planes and zeppelins, rigid airships filled with nitrogen gas and propelled by powerful engines, dropped bombs on soldiers and civilians.

British citizen John Agnew witnessed firsthand the damage the air war could do. In January 1915, he watched as a German zeppelin dropped bombs on his neighborhood.

The explosion of bombs signaled the approach of the German airship. Within a few moments I heard the noise of the airship's propellers and a little later saw the Zeppelin against the sky. The airship, approaching from the east, circled the town, dropping four bombs. . . . The third bomb was the only one that resulted in casualties. It fell in Bentinick Street and killed a lad asleep in his bed, at the same time burying the boy's father, mother and baby sister in the debris of the home.[1]

The first American airmen were volunteers who served with the French Air Force in 1916. The pilots of the Lafayette Escadrille, called "knights of the air," were idolized as heroes in the United States. The Americans began training pilots in 1917 and had nine thousand by the end of 1918. Most of these student pilots were thrilled to be in the air. "It's a great life, mother, flying alone with nothing to worry about, the whole sky to fly in, and not much work to do," wrote student pilot Allan Parr. "I will really hate to see this old war stop, if it ever does. I am having such a fine time."[2]

Once in France, American pilots quickly learned how dangerous their mission could be. They flew without parachutes in rickety planes made of cloth and canvas that could rip apart in a sharp dive or turn. The German aviators were well trained and battle hardened. Pilot life expectancy on the western front was measured in just weeks. Even Raoul Lufbery, one of the finest American pilots, who had shot down seventeen German aircraft, could not outrun the odds. Captain Eddie Rickenbacker, the most famous American pilot of the war, saw Lufbery's luck run out in an air fight known as a dogfight on May 19, 1918.

> Luf[bery] fired several short-bursts as he dived in to the attack [on a German fighter plane]. Then he swerved away and appeared to busy himself with his gun, which evidently had jammed. Another circle over their heads and he had cleared the jam. Again he rushed the enemy from their rear, when suddenly old Luf's machine was seen to burst into roaring flames. . . . Then to the horrified watchers below there appeared the figure of their gallant hero emerging in a headlong leap from the midst of the fiery furnace!

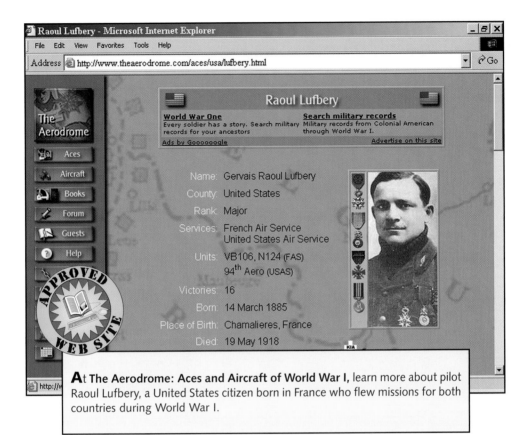

At The Aerodrome: Aces and Aircraft of World War I, learn more about pilot Raoul Lufbery, a United States citizen born in France who flew missions for both countries during World War I.

Lufbery had preferred a leap to certain death rather than endure the slow torture of burning to a crisp. His body fell in the garden of a [French] peasant woman's house in a little town.[3]

While aerial warfare in World War I had little impact on the war's outcome, it did pave the way for the terrible air battles of World War II.

▶ Supplying the Troops

Of the millions of Americans who served in the war, most never saw combat. Many were put to work getting supplies from the United States to the front lines. By 1918, an amazing two hundred thousand tons of supplies were being unloaded every month in one French port alone. Much of this backbreaking supply work was done by black soldiers. General James Harbord told how efficiently these men could move supplies:

> [A] telegram was received one morning at 8:15 order-ing exactly 4,596 tons of supplies which were to comprise 1,250,000 cans of tomatoes; 1,000,000 pound of dry beans. By 6:15 that evening, this demand had been filled and 457 freight cars were loaded with it and on their way to [the trenches].[4]

Huge kitchens had to be set up to prepare cooked food for the troops. A single bakery made an astounding 750,000 pounds of bread every day.[5] One of the most dangerous missions of the war was getting these food rations up to the front over open ground in horse-drawn carts at night when they were often shelled or machine-gunned.

▶ Women at War

Though no American women were allowed to fight in World War I, they played a vital role behind the lines in France. Over thirty thousand women served in the Army and Navy Nurse Corps. Many more American women served with the Red Cross, the Young Men's Christian Association (YMCA), or the

Salvation Army as volunteers, acting as nurses or providing food to the troops.

Three U.S. Army nurses won the Distinguished Service Medal, the nation's second highest military honor. One of them, Helen Fairchild, died in the war. Here, chief nurse Julia Stimson tells of the difficult conditions under which Fairchild and other nurses often worked.

[W]hat with the steam, the ether, and the filthy clothes of the [wounded] men ... the odor in the operating room was so terrible that it was all any of

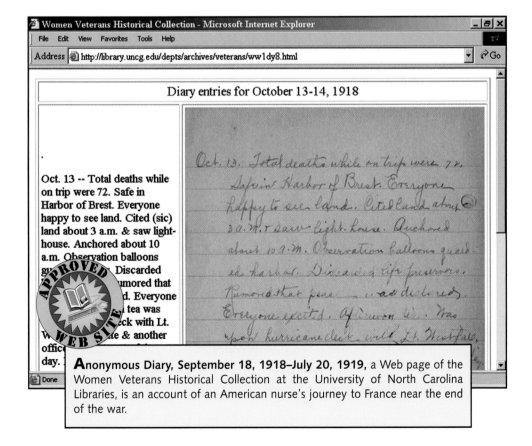

Women Veterans Historical Collection - Microsoft Internet Explorer

File   Edit   View   Favorites   Tools   Help

Address   http://library.uncg.edu/depts/archives/veterans/ww1dy8.html   Go

Diary entries for October 13-14, 1918

Oct. 13 -- Total deaths while on trip were 72. Safe in Harbor of Brest. Everyone happy to see land. Cited (sic) land about 3 a.m. & saw light-house. Anchored about 10 a.m. Observation balloons gu... Discarded ... umored that ... d. Everyone ... tea was ... ck with Lt. ... te & another ... office... day.

Anonymous Diary, September 18, 1918–July 20, 1919, a Web page of the Women Veterans Historical Collection at the University of North Carolina Libraries, is an account of an American nurse's journey to France near the end of the war.

them [the nurses] could do to keep from being sick
. . . no mere handling of instruments and sponges, but
sewing and tying up and putting in drains while the
doctor takes the next piece of shell out of another
place. Then after fourteen hours of this with freezing
feet, to a meal of tea and bread and jam, then off to
rest if you can, in a wet bell tent in a damp bed without sheets, after a wash with a cupful of water . . . one
need never tell me that women can't do as much,
stand as much, and be as brave as men.[6]

Nurse Marion Rice was horrified by her inability
to help the most severely wounded.

[Y]ou never smelled such smells or saw such sights. I
can't tell you how many amputations there were. . . .
One man has both legs gone, he lay in a shell hole six
days, there was nothing to eat but the hole was filled
with water and in that water lay decaying the body of
his best friend. And he had to drink that water to keep
alive. Pleasant isn't it. Such wrecks as many of these
men are such [brave] faces . . . but I am afraid there
will be some who will never go out the front door
[alive].[7]

Other women worked near the front, including
"Hello Girls," who spoke both French and English,
and served as phone operators. One "Hello Girl"
complained that men got all the headlines, that she
never read a word in the newspapers about the "250
girls who plug from morning until night, who
scream their lungs out to trenches over [phone]
lines that are tied to trees, to fence-posts, and along

the ground. Not that we care. We came over here to do our work . . . help the boys . . . [and] get the Kaiser."[8]

Digitized Primary American History Sources

Access this Web site from http://www.myreportlinks.com

This University of Northern Iowa archive offers links to primary source collections on the Web. Scroll down to find links to primary source materials about World War I.

It was the crucially important service of American women in World War I that helped give the final push to pass the Nineteenth Amendment to the Constitution in August 1920. That amendment barred discrimination on the basis of sex, so women were finally allowed to vote in elections. Woodrow Wilson had opposed the amendment at first but then recognized the key role women had played in the war. "We have made partners of the women in this war," said the president. "Shall we admit them only to a partnership of suffering and sacrifice and toil, and not to a partnership of privilege and right?"[9]

▶ Serving Europe After the War's End

The fighting ended on November 11, 1918, with the signing of the armistice. That did not mean that American men and women serving in France could come home right away. After the guns stopped firing and everyone stopped celebrating, there was much work to do. Some soldiers helped the French rebuild towns or roads across the shell-torn landscape.

Other troops were sent to occupy defeated Germany. Many doughboys were surprised by the welcome they received there. Sergeant William Argall wrote:

I'll never forget the morning we marched into that German town. . . . We expected the Germans to treat us with scorn and be utterly indifferent and even nasty with us but we surely got the surprise of our lives, when as we marched through the main street of the town we were greeted by the entire populace. . . . [T]he German girls marched ahead of us and strewed our path with wreaths of flowers of every description.[10]

Some soldiers found it hard to hate those who had been their enemy. Captain Arthur Hyde wrote to his sister, saying, "It is next to impossible for me to scowl at the timid, pretty German children with their round eyes and yellow hair . . . or to act haughty to the deferential [polite] grown-ups as they cringingly lift their hats as I pass."[11]

But soon, the soldiers who had endured so many hardships during the war tired of their boring duties and the discipline of army life. They just wanted to go home. With the war over, Lieutenant Watson Avery complained, "I have no idea what we will do [next], where we will go, or most important of all how long we will be on this side of the pond [a reference to the Atlantic Ocean]."[12]

Another soldier, Sergeant Aksel Olson, wrote home: "I hate this life [occupying Germany] with all that is in me. . . . There is nothing here to live for

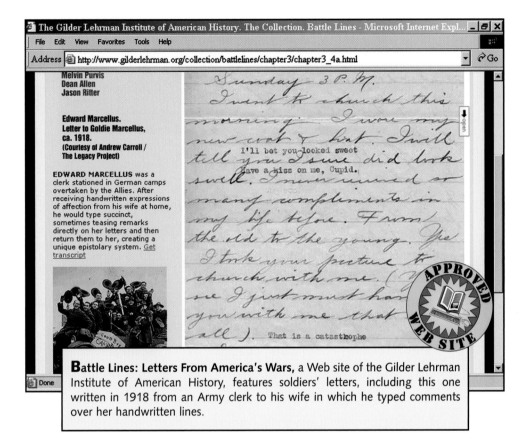

The Gilder Lehrman Institute of American History. The Collection. Battle Lines - Microsoft Internet Expl... _ ⎕ ✕

File   Edit   View   Favorites   Tools   Help

Address ☒ http://www.gilderlehrman.org/collection/battlelines/chapter3/chapter3_4a.html   ▼ ⟳ Go

Melvin Purvis
Dean Allen
Jason Ritter

**Edward Marcellus.
Letter to Goldie Marcellus,
ca. 1918.**
(Courtesy of Andrew Carroll /
The Legacy Project)

EDWARD MARCELLUS was a clerk stationed in German camps overtaken by the Allies. After receiving handwritten expressions of affection from his wife at home, he would type succinct, sometimes teasing remarks directly on her letters and then return them to her, creating a unique epistolary system. Get transcript

Battle Lines: Letters From America's Wars, a Web site of the Gilder Lehrman Institute of American History, features soldiers' letters, including this one written in 1918 from an Army clerk to his wife in which he typed comments over her handwritten lines.

that I can see. . . . Our job is ended and everyone wishes to go home."[13]

All the doughboys could talk about was what they would do when they got out of the army. Sergeant Neil W. Kimball told how one soldier wanted "to take his rifle with him when he is mustered out [able to leave the army]. He is going to stand it up under the drain spout and watch it rust."[14] The Americans finally came home in 1919.

THE WAR AT HOME

The men who fought in the First World War were changed by the experience, and when they returned home, they found a different United States as well. World War I had brought dramatic changes on the home front. With the country at war, freedoms guaranteed under the U.S. Constitution were reduced, and German-American citizens were sometimes attacked. Providing weapons for war led to a boom in manufacturing. This boom helped women and minorities get jobs that had once been available only to white males.

▶ War or No War?

Many accounts of World War I say that the majority of Americans wanted to go to war. The truth is, no one really knows. In 1917, there was no way to measure public opinion accurately. What is known is that many people supported the war, especially in the government, while many, especially among farmers and laborers and the growing immigrant population of German, Italian, and Irish, opposed it.

President Wilson did his best to use patriotism to inspire Americans to fight when he asked for a

This poster from 1917 is a call for America, symbolized by a sleeping woman, to "wake up" and support the war effort.

declaration of war against Germany on April 2, 1917.

We are now about to accept . . . battle with [Germany] this natural foe to liberty and shall . . . fight thus for the ultimate peace of the world and for the liberation of its peoples, the German peoples included: for the rights of nations great and small and the privilege of men everywhere to choose their way of life. . . . The world must be made safe for democracy.[1]

Eugene Debs, head of the Socialist party in the United States, had a different point of view. His political party called the declaration of war "a crime against the people of the United States."[2] Debs's objection was his belief that the poor workers of all nations were being forced to fight each other so that rich weapon makers and bankers of all nations could profit. He continued this line of thought in a speech.

Wars throughout history have been waged for conquest and plunder. . . . And that is war in a nutshell. The master class has always declared the wars, the subject class has always fought the battles. . . . If war is right let it be declared by the people [and not by the president and Congress]. You [the people] who have your lives to lose, you certainly above all others have the right to decide the momentous issue of war or peace.[3]

▷ Limiting Freedom

Fearing that the words of war protesters might hurt the war effort, the U.S. government imprisoned Debs and nine hundred other protest leaders under the Espionage Act, passed by Congress in 1917. According to this act, anyone who spoke against the war "shall be punished by a fine of not more than $10,000 or imprisonment for not more than twenty years, or both."[4]

Though the Espionage Act was supposed to catch spies, it often resulted in the jailing of people who voiced their First Amendment right to free speech. A South Dakota farmer named Fred Fairchild was jailed for a year for saying, "If I were of conscription age . . . and were drafted, I would refuse to serve. They could shoot me, but they could not make me fight."[5]

In 1917, George Creel, a newspaperman, was appointed the head of the U.S. Committee on Public Information. In this role, he headed the American

The Four-Minute Men were part of the American government's publicity campaign during the war to promote America's involvement. This poster comes from the **World War I Poster Collection Guide,** a college Web site.

government's propaganda and publicity agency—his job was to get Americans to back the war. Creel recruited and trained seventy-five thousand volunteers, known as the "Four-Minute Men," to speak around the nation. They gave thousands of brief speeches in favor of the war, like the following, which asked Americans to provide a huge loan to pay for the war:

Ladies and Gentlemen: I have just received the information that there is a German spy among *us*— a German spy watching us. He is around, here somewhere, reporting upon you and me—sending reports about us to Berlin and telling the Germans just what we are doing with the Liberty Loan. . . . For the German Government is worried about our great loan. . . . If the American people lend their billions now, one and all with a hip-hip-hurrah, it means that America is united and strong. While, if we lend our money half-heartedly, America seems weak. . . . Money means everything now; it means quicker victory and therefore less bloodshed. We are *in* the war, and now Americans can have but *one* opinion [which is to support the war].[6]

Thirteen million men backed the war by registering for the draft. More than 330,000 men evaded the draft, and 65,000 declared themselves conscientious objectors, or COs. They refused to fight on moral or religious grounds, and many were jailed for their beliefs. One anonymous CO said after the war:

Dont kid yourself, nor let anyone else kid you, about the C.O's being afraid of fighting; it took a damned sight more guts to resist the national [war] hysteria than to fall in line with it. . . . [T]here were times when we had no more assurance of emerging alive from the jails and penitentiaries than were the more glorified and subserviant guys in the trenches.[7]

With war protest silenced, the United States government propaganda machine used military bands, parades, celebrity spokespeople, war-bond rallies, patriotic movies, posters, and pamphlets to keep support for the war strong.

Building the First Arsenal of Democracy

From 1914 until 1917, though the United States was supposed to be neutral, American manufacturers sold large amounts of weapons to Britain. Banks such as J. P. Morgan & Company loaned millions of dollars to the British.

When the United States finally declared war, industry mobilized to provide supplies and weapons. Frank Vanderlip, president of the National City Bank of New York, understood the need:

> We ought clearly to comprehend that this is a war of equipment. Our men may be as brave as any heros ever were, but they cannot successfully fight this sort of fight barehanded. They must have the equipment of guns great and small, of ammunition, of a sky full of airplanes, and of a bridge of ships across the Atlantic.[8]

With industry booming and men going to war, women and African Americans were able to get jobs in steel mills and munitions plants. Many black men and women gave up their work in the south as servants or farmhands and moved north in what became known as the Great Migration. Writer Frank

Boyd described this exodus from the rural south to the more industrialized north:

> At that time, there was a great demand for cheap industrial labor. Strongbacked, physically capable Negroes from the South were the answer to this demand. They came North in droves, beginning what turned out to be the greatest migration of Negroes in the history of the United States. The good news about jobs spread like wildfire throughout the Southlands. There was money, good money, to be made in the [industrial] North, especially New York, New York; the wonder, the magic city.[9]

American Leaders Speak: Recordings From World War I and the 1920 Election, a Library of Congress Web site, provides audio clips of American leaders from World War I and the postwar election of 1920, including one of Frank Vanderlip. His speech implored Americans to forego luxuries and conserve materials to "save the lives of American soldiers."

For skilled machinists such as Italian-American Charles Fusco, arming for the war brought prosperity, though unfortunately many workers lost their jobs when peace came.

> America went in [to the war] and we started to make the Brownie [Browning] machine gun. . . . the whole factory started in to make them. . . . I got 65 cents an hour and there was others that was making 50 to 60 dollars a week. Boys 17 and 18 years old. . . . [but] After the war everybody got laid off . . .[10]

A weekly salary of fifty to sixty dollars was a lot of money at the time.

▶ Women on the Home Front

Before World War I, most women worked at home cooking, cleaning, and rearing their children. During the war, a million women who had never been allowed to work in "men's jobs" suddenly found themselves recruited for such positions. As one newspaper reported:

> There has been a sudden influx of women into such unusual occupations as bank clerks, ticket sellers, elevator operator, chauffeur, street car conductor, railroad trackwalker, section hand, locomotive wiper and oiler, locomotive dispatcher, block operator, draw bridge attendant, and employment in machine shops, steel mills, powder and ammunition factories, airplane works, boot blacking and farming.[11]

Many of these women were paid at half the rate of men doing the same jobs, although that had been true for working women even before the war. Many women also worked long hours at dangerous work, such as filling artillery shells with explosives. Still, the importance of working women to the war effort helped the suffragist movement, which had been striving for decades to get women the vote. Suffragist Harriot Stanton Blatch borrowed phrases from the war to describe women's advances.

American women have begun to go over the top. They are going up the [career] scaling-ladder and out into

▲ Suffragists from Washington, D.C., picket in New York City in December 1917.

File   Edit   View   Favorites   Tools   Help

Address http://memory.loc.gov/cgi-bin/np_item.pl   Go

The New York Times

ture Section,
gravure: Part 1

The New York Times

Sunday,
October 31, 181

Page 4 of 12

Next

er 31, 1915

Newspaper Pictorials: World War I Rotogravures, a Web site of the Library of Congress, provides a collection of high-quality illustrations reprinted by newspapers form the era. Here, a women's suffrage parade appears on the front page of the *New York Times.*

All Man's Land. . . . America is witnessing the beginning of a great industrial and social change. . . . There is not an occupation in which a woman is not found. When men go a-warring, women go to work.[12]

Women's suffrage groups supported the war effort in the hope that women would finally be allowed to vote. Members of the National Women's party picketed the White House, and some were jailed for demanding that the democracy for which the country was fighting overseas be extended to women at home. In 1920, Congress ratified the

Nineteenth Amendment, which finally gave women the vote: "The right of citizens of the United States to vote shall not be denied or abridged by the United States or by any State on account of sex."[13]

Though most women gave up their jobs after the soldiers came home, World War I advanced women's rights in the United States.

Attacks on German Americans

One of the most troubling events on the home front was the accusation of disloyalty against German Americans. Anti-German hysteria caused familiar German terms such as "frankfurter" and "sauerkraut" to be changed to "hot dog" and "liberty cabbage." German music was banned by some orchestras, and the teaching of the German language was even dropped by some schools. Fearful German Americans sometimes anglicized their

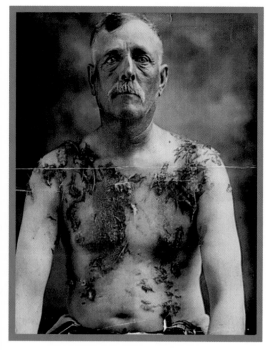

Anti-German sentiments were widespread in the United States during World War I, and some Americans of German descent were treated harshly in the name of national security. John Meintz was tarred and feathered for refusing to support war-bond drives.

names, changing "Schmidt" to "Smith," for example. While most German immigrants were not imprisoned, as Japanese Americans would be during World War II, some people suspected them of supporting Germany, and some of those people were people in power. Judge George C. Webb wildly exaggerated when he said, "There is not a state in the Union that is not infested with German spies, and they do not hesitate at anything to spread German propaganda, which is the most villainous, barbarous, and extensive menace that the country has to cope with."[14] Congressman Julius Kahn of California declared, "I hope that we shall have a few prompt hangings [of German Americans] and the sooner the better. We have got to make an example of a few of these people, and we have got to do it quickly."[15]

Shortly after this remark, an innocent German-American immigrant named Robert Prager was stripped of his clothes, bound with an American flag, and lynched by a drunken mob. Several thousand German Americans were unfairly imprisoned, and others lost their United States citizenship. Despite the hysteria, not one German American was ever found to be a spy, and German-American doughboys served bravely in the war on the side of the Allies.

THE WAR IN SONG AND LITERATURE

World War I, like other wars, had an influence on the culture of the time. Songs, poems, and novels were written about almost every aspect of the Great War.

▷ Songs of War and Peace

Most World War I songs favored the war, but not all. Two of the most popular songs in the United States were the antiwar song "I Didn't Raise My Boy to Be a Soldier" and the pro-war song "Over There."

By 1915, Americans were debating whether to go to war or not. Many members of the Socialist party and German Americans were against the war then. "I Didn't Raise My Boy to Be a Soldier" expressed a mother's doubts about joining in Europe's war.

Ten million soldiers to the war have gone,
Who may never return again.
Ten million mothers' hearts must break,
For the ones who died in vain.
Head bowed down in sorrow in her lonely years,
I heard a mother murmur thro' her tears:

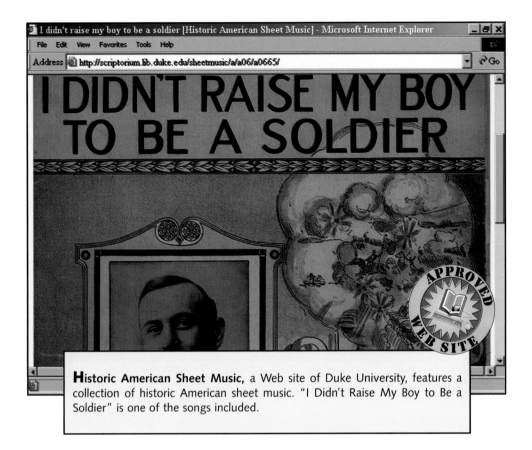

Historic American Sheet Music, a Web site of Duke University, features a collection of historic American sheet music. "I Didn't Raise My Boy to Be a Soldier" is one of the songs included.

Chorus:

I didn't raise my boy to be a soldier,
I brought him up to be my pride and joy,
Who dares to place a musket on his shoulder,
To shoot some other mother's darling boy?[1]

When America entered the war in 1917, the popular songwriter George M. Cohan wrote "Over There," which became the biggest hit of World War I. It was sung everywhere, and its appeal to patriotism helped with the troop recruitment effort.

Johnnie, get your gun,

Get your gun, get your gun,

Take it on the run,

On the run, on the run.

Hear them calling, you and me,

Every son of liberty.

Hurry right away,

No delay, no delay,

Make your daddy glad

To have had such a lad.

Tell your sweetheart not to pine,

To be proud her boy's in line.

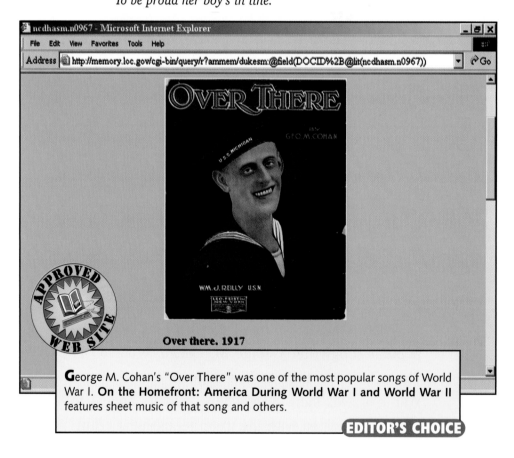

Over there. 1917

George M. Cohan's "Over There" was one of the most popular songs of World War I. **On the Homefront: America During World War I and World War II** features sheet music of that song and others.

EDITOR'S CHOICE

Johnnie, get your gun,

Get your gun, get your gun,

Johnnie show the Hun

Who's a son of a gun.

Hoist the flag and let her fly,

Yankee Doodle do or die.

Pack your little kit,

Show your grit, do your bit.

Yankee Doodle fill the ranks,

From the towns and the tanks.

Make your mother proud of you,

And the old Red, White and Blue.

Over there, over there,

Send the word, send the word over there—

That the Yanks are coming,

The Yanks are coming,

The drums rum-tumming

Ev'rywhere.

So prepare, say a pray'r,

Send the word, send the word to beware.

We'll be over, we're coming over,

And we won't come back till it's over

Over there.[2]

Hundreds of other pro-war songs were written, including "Keep the Home Fires Burning," a call to fight and endure the suffering of war. This song, written in 1914 when Britain went to war, became popular in America when it joined the fight.

*They were summoned from the hillside, they were
    called in from the glen,*

*And the country found them ready at the stirring call
    for men.*

*Let no tears add to their hardships, as the soldiers pass
    along,*

*And although your heart is breaking, make it sing this
    cheery song:*

Keep the Home Fires Burning,

While your hearts are yearning,

Though your lads are far away they dream of home.

There's a silver lining, through the dark clouds shining,

Turn the dark cloud inside out, 'til the boys come home.[3]

Antiwar songs were less well known. In this
song, a little girl pleaded, "Don't Take My Papa Away
From Me."

*Don't take my papa away from me, don't leave me
    there all alone.*

*He has cared for me so tenderly, ever since mother
    was gone.*

*Nobody ever like him can be, no one can so with
    me play.*

*Don't take my papa away from me; please don't take
    papa away.*

Sentimental songs such as "Keep the Home Fires Burning" asked those on the home front to bear up while waiting for their "boys" at war, like this American pilot, to return.

Her tender pleadings were all in vain, and her father
    went to the war.

He'll never kiss her good night again, for he fell 'mid
    the cannon's roar.

Greater a soldier was never born, but his brave heart
    was pierced one day;

And as he was dying, he heard some one crying,
    A girl's voice from far away.[4]

Lieutenant James Reese Europe was the leader of the all-black 369th Infantry "Harlem Hellfighters" Band. A jazz musician, his song "On Patrol in No Man's Land" offers a firsthand account of the dangers of a trench raid and has a similar rhyming style to that found in modern rap music:

What the time? Nine?

Fall in line

Alright, boys, now take it slow

Are you ready? Steady!

Very good, Eddie.

Over the top, let's go

Quiet, lie it, else you'll start a riot

Keep your proper distance, follow 'long

Cover, brother, and when you see me hover

Obey my orders and you won't go wrong

There's a Minenwerfer [German mortar] coming—

look out (bang!)

Hear that roar (bang!), there's one more (bang!)

Stand fast, there's a Very light [flare]

James Reese Europe and his Harlem Hellfighters introduced jazz to France, where it has remained popular ever since.

Don't gasp or they'll find you all right

Don't start to bombing with those hand grenades

   (rat-a-tat-tat-tat)

There's a machine gun, holy spades!

Alert, gas! Put on your mask

Adjust it correctly and hurry up fast

Drop! There's a rocket from the Boche barrage

Down, hug the ground, close as you can, don't stand

Creep and crawl, follow me, that's all

What do you hear? Nothing near

Don't fear, all is clear

That's the life of a stroll

When you take a patrol

Out in No Man's Land

Ain't it grand?

Out in No Man's Land.[5]

▶ Wartime Poets

British war poets wrote the best-known poems of World War I, but America had its own soldier-poets. One was Alan Seeger, who volunteered to fight in the British Army before America entered the war. Seeger wrote in his last letter home, "We go up to the attack tomorrow. This will probably be the biggest thing yet. . . . I am glad to be going in [the] first wave. If you are in this thing at all it is best to be in to the limit. And this is the supreme experience."[6] Seeger died shortly thereafter. His poem "Rendezvous" fore-told his own death on the battlefield.

I have a rendezvous with Death
At some disputed barricade, . . .
It may be he shall take my hand
And lead me into his dark land
And close my eyes and quench my breath—
It may be I shall pass him still.
I have a rendezvous with Death
On some scarred slope of battered hill,
When Spring comes round again this year
And the first meadow-flowers appear.[7]

AEF officer John Allan Wyeth wrote poems that evoked the daily horror of trench warfare. His poem *La Voie Sacree,* "The Sacred Route," is about a soldier who tries to take shelter for the night in a house destroyed by artillery, only to be awakened by a rat that has chewed through his pocket.

These houses died too long ago to care
who comes and echoes in their empty shells.
Our broken rooms stay blank and vacant still
although we laughed and talked an hour or two.
Rats squeak and scrabble brusquely everywhere.
The night is almost blind . . . Something dispels
my stupor, wakes me with a squeamish thrill
to find my raincoat pocket eaten through . . .[8]

Not all war poems were written by soldiers. Ella Wheeler Wilcox wrote a book saluting the dough-boys, including a poem celebrating the role of Army stevedores, dockworkers who unloaded ships:

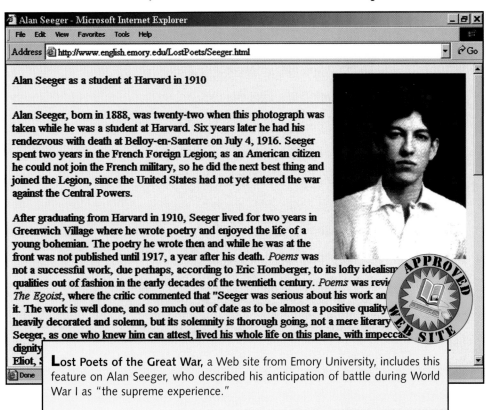

Alan Seeger - Microsoft Internet Explorer

File   Edit   View   Favorites   Tools   Help

Address http://www.english.emory.edu/LostPoets/Seeger.html   Go

Alan Seeger as a student at Harvard in 1910

Alan Seeger, born in 1888, was twenty-two when this photograph was taken while he was a student at Harvard. Six years later he had his rendezvous with death at Belloy-en-Santerre on July 4, 1916. Seeger spent two years in the French Foreign Legion; as an American citizen he could not join the French military, so he did the next best thing and joined the Legion, since the United States had not yet entered the war against the Central Powers.

After graduating from Harvard in 1910, Seeger lived for two years in Greenwich Village where he wrote poetry and enjoyed the life of a young bohemian. The poetry he wrote then and while he was at the front was not published until 1917, a year after his death. *Poems* was not a successful work, due perhaps, according to Eric Homberger, to its lofty idealism, qualities out of fashion in the early decades of the twentieth century. *Poems* was revi *The Egoist*, where the critic commented that "Seeger was serious about his work an it. The work is well done, and so much out of date as to be almost a positive quality heavily decorated and solemn, but its solemnity is thorough going, not a mere literary Seeger, as one who knew him can attest, lived his whole life on this plane, with impecc dignity

Eliot,

Done

Lost Poets of the Great War, a Web site from Emory University, includes this feature on Alan Seeger, who described his anticipation of battle during World War I as "the supreme experience."

We are the army stevedores, lusty and virile and
    strong,
We are given the hardest work of the war, and the
    hours are long.
We handle the heavy boxes, and shovel the dirty coal;
While soldiers and sailors work in the light, we
    burrow below like a mole.

But somebody has to do this work, or the soldiers
    could not fight!
And whatever work is given a man, is good if he
    does it right. . . .
We are the army stevedores, and work as we must
    and may,
The cross of honour will never be ours to proudly
    wear away.

But the men at the Front could never be there,
And the battles could not be won,
If the stevedores stopped in their dull routine
And left their work undone.
Somebody has to do this work, be glad that it
    isn't you!
We are the army stevedores—give us our due![9]

▶ The Lost Generation

Many who fought and survived World War I suffered
deep psychological scars for the rest of their lives.
These veterans were disillusioned by the absurdity
and meaninglessness of modern war. Some who came
home were bitter at seeing so many friends die without knowing what they died for. These embittered
veterans were called the Lost Generation.

One such man, Lieutenant Curtis Kinney, asked: "Was it our fight? Indeed, was it anyone's fight?" Kinney's despair is reflected in his poem "1918":

> We flew together
> In the tall blue sky.
> We fought together
> With bombs and gains [guns].
> We ate together
> In the squadron mess.
> We danced together
> To the old gramophone.
> We walked together
> In the fields of France.
> We talked together
> Of home and tomorrow.
> We flew together
> In the tall blue sky.
> Many were killed;
> The world is no better.[10]

Most famous among the Lost Generation were two veterans, one from each side, who wrote novels about the waste of war. American Ernest Hemingway and German Erich Maria Remarque wrote two of the most read antiwar novels. Remarque's book *All Quiet on the Western Front* was written in 1927 and was so highly thought of in America that it was made into a successful film. Remarque had fought in the German Army on the western front where he was wounded several times. His book's main character is teenager Paul Bäumer, who with his friends is encouraged to go to war by their schoolteacher. Instead of war being glorious, as the teacher promised, Bäumer and his pals find World War I to be brutal, terrifying, and pointless.

The war has ruined us for everything. . . . We are not youth any longer. . . . We were eighteen and had begun to love life and the world; and we had to shoot it to pieces. The first bomb, the first explosion, burst in our hearts. We are cut off from activity, from striving, from progress. We believe in such things no longer, we believe in the war.[11]

At one point, Bäumer finds himself in a shell hole with an enemy soldier whom he kills. Trapped with the corpse, Bäumer begins to see his enemy as a friend.

[N]ow, for the first time, I see you are a man like me. I thought of your hand-grenades, of your bayonet, of your rifle; now I see your wife and your face and our fellowship. Forgive me, comrade. We always see it too late. Why do they never tell us that you are just poor devils like us, that your mothers are just as anxious as ours, and that we have the same fear of death, and the same dying and the same agony—Forgive me, comrade; how could you be my enemy. If we threw away these rifles and this uniform you could be my brother. . . .[12]

Ernest Hemingway's novel *A Farewell to Arms,* written in 1929, is based on the writer's own experiences as a young ambulance driver in Italy during the war. It tells the story of Lieutenant Frederic Henry, who also serves in the Italian Army during

World War I. Henry sees a great deal of death, is wounded, and is finally nauseated by the barbarity of war. He deserts the army and flees the fighting. At one point, Henry worries that World War I will never end and may last a hundred years. "Perhaps wars weren't won anymore," he muses. "Maybe they went on forever."[13] Though this seems like an exaggeration, wars were fought continuously at different places in the twentieth century. Henry also doubts the "noble" reasons that nations give for going to war.

FirstWorldWar.com

Access this Web site from http://www.myreportlinks.com

The FirstWorldWar.com Web site houses an extensive collection of primary source documents of World War I, including some of the poetry of Ernest Hemingway.

I was always embarrassed by the words sacred, glorious, and sacrifice. . . . We [soldiers] had heard them, sometimes [in speeches] standing in the rain almost out of earshot, so that only the shouted words came through, and had read them, on [government] proclamations . . . I had seen nothing sacred [in war], and the things that were glorious had no glory and the sacrifices [of dying soldiers] were like the stockyards at Chicago if nothing was done with the meat except to bury it. There were many words that you could not stand to hear [after having fought in the Great War]. . . . Abstract words such as glory, honor, courage, or hallow were obscene. . . .[14]

PRESS COVERAGE AND PROPAGANDA

Neither radio nor television existed in 1917, so most Americans learned about the war from newspapers. While many periodicals supported the war, there were some magazines that opposed it.

▷ The Mainstream Press

Once the United States entered World War I, most major American newspapers joined in supporting the war. They reported the news, but they were also biased toward the United States and against Germany. For example, the Battle of Belleau Wood was fought heroically by both sides, but newspaper accounts made it sound as if the U.S. Marines were winning easily over demoralized and cowardly Germans. Compare this *New York Times* account of the battle with the accounts of doughboys from the first chapter in this book.

> At the nearer edge of the woods, devastated by our shellfire, they [the Marines] encountered little opposition. A little further on the Germans made a small stand, but were completely routed. . . . By this time the marines were fairly started on their way. They swept forward, clearing out machine gun nests with rifle fire, bayonets, and hand grenades. . . . The

Germans started in headlong flight when the Americans seized two machine guns and turned them on the Germans with terrific effect. The Germans soon tired of this, and those nearest the Americans began surrendering. . . .[1]

A *Washington Post* article carried this obviously biased headline about the German Army commander Paul von Hindenburg:

HIGHLIGHTS IN THE CAREER OF HINDENBURG THE HUN . . . the Man Who Heralded Himself as "the Biggest Liar in Germany"—His Religion Is Cruelty, His

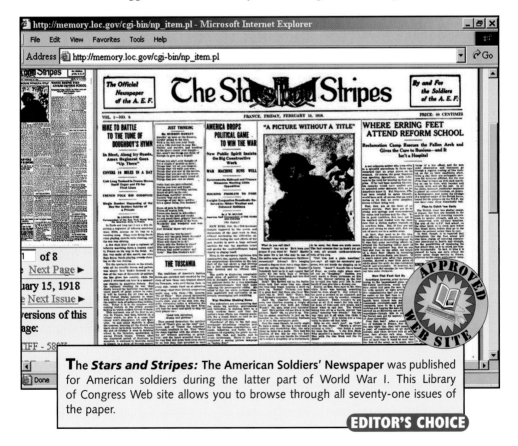

The **Stars and Stripes: The American Soldiers' Newspaper** was published for American soldiers during the latter part of World War I. This Library of Congress Web site allows you to browse through all seventy-one issues of the paper.

EDITOR'S CHOICE

Soul Is That of a Mongolian, He Has No Manners and
He Detests the Kaiser.

The writer of this propaganda piece goes on to
say that Hindenburg's appearance is "gorilla-like,"
and "To meet Von Hindenburg once was an experience to be remembered no less vividly than an
encounter with the semi-human brute of the African
jungle." The same article features a picture of German
soldiers bayoneting and strangling civilians, with
the caption, "When they can no longer resist, you
enslave them!"[2]

Life Goes On

Newspapers covered the daily happenings on the
home front as well as news from the front lines, and
the two made for a strange combination. The week
of August 4, 1918, the Allies launched a number of
hammering attacks against the Germans that would
help end the war. The *Washington Post* reported that
momentous news on page 1 with the headline
"GREAT SALIENT WIPED OUT . . . More than 50
Towns Occupied by Allies; Fleeing Huns Lose
Heavily . . . Begin New Retreat."[3] Just below this
headline was a local piece of news that had nothing
to do with the war: "2 POLICE SHOT BY PAY-ROLL
BANDITS."[4] Inside the paper were advertisements
for Goldheim's clothing store, which was having a
sale on three-piece wool suits for as little as $25, and
O. J. DeMoll & Co., selling phonographs for $115.[5]

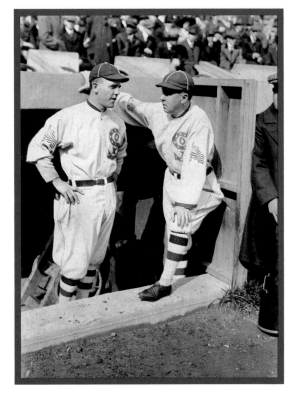

Clarence "Pants" Rowland, (right) Chicago White Sox manager, speaks to Eddie Cicotte, his pitcher, in a photograph taken between 1915 and 1918. Despite the war, Americans' love of baseball, the national pastime, continued.

In the Help Wanted section, jobs ranging from pot washer to typist were advertised. Some ads specified the race of the person desired—now an illegal practice. One announced "WAR WORK—White girls over 15 for work in manufacturing department for various equipment."[6] There was such a shortage of men that white teenage girls were being hired as wartime industrial workers.

Life as usual could also be seen in the continued interest in sports: The war never interrupted the reporting of sports news. The big sports story on August 4, 1918, in the *Washington Post* highlighted a baseball game between the Washington Nationals and the Detroit Tigers: "Washington batting averages went up as high as the thermometer around the equator this afternoon, with four Detroit pitchers making abbreviated sojourns on the mound."[7]

Human-interest stories that highlighted the work done on the home front in support of the war often made the news. One such story on August 8 told of an elderly woman's prowess in knitting socks for soldiers: "HOLDS SOCKS RECORD" blared the headline.

Alexandria woman, Aged 83, Now Knitting Her 111th Pair. . . . Mrs. Edward J. Evans Has a Son Who Is a Captain in France and Has a Grandson Who Is a Lieutenant—Father was "Fighting Parson" in Revolutionary War.[8]

▶ The Alternative Press

The American publications that opposed the war included the *Mother Earth Journal,* the *Messenger,* and the *Masses.* These magazines were tolerated by the government until Congress declared war. After that, the government tried to shut them—and other antiwar publications—down.

Cartoons were among the strongest weapons of the *Masses.* "Conscription" showed a draftee being measured for a uniform by Death, represented by a skeleton.[9] Another cartoon showed a mother chimpanzee and her son. The young chimp, after throwing down a newspaper emblazoned with the headline "WAR," says, "Mother, never let me hear you tell the children that these humans are descendants of ours."[10] Still another cartoon showed Jesus Christ wearing prison stripes. Its caption read, "The prisoner used language tending to discourage men from enlisting in the United States Army. It is proven and indeed admitted that among his incendiary statements were—Thou shalt not kill and Blessed are the peacemakers."[11]

Attorney and writer Harry Weinberger defended the right to free speech in time of war in *Mother Earth Journal,* a magazine that was shut down by the government.

> Men and women in America are going to jail for having ideals and consciences and for expressing their opinions for terms longer than they gave in Russia for the same offenses under the Tsar. And always the plea is "necessity of War." History shows that the plea is always some "necessity" to prevent human thought and progress.[12]

Some African-American writers also questioned the war. In the *Messenger,* editor and writer Philip Randolph asked why black doughboys and factory workers should fight for democracy in Europe while their civil rights were still being denied at home.

> [W]e are conscripting [drafting] the Negro into the military and industrial establishments to achieve . . . white democracy four thousand miles away, while the Negro at home, though bearing the burden [of war] in

every way, is denied economic, political, educational and civil democracy.[13]

Patriotism or Propaganda?

Americans on the home front were reminded of the war by government posters displayed prominently in public places in towns and cities across the country. Many posters appealed strongly to the emotions rather than to facts, and as such were propaganda. But their use was practical, as well. The pictures on posters helped convince recent immigrants, many from eastern and southern Europe who could not speak or read English, to support the war effort. The posters were also used to persuade many Irish immigrants to fight on the Allies' side despite their anti-British sentiments.

The most famous war poster of the time, created by James Montgomery Flagg, showed Uncle Sam, a figure used to symbolize the United States, in a red, white, and blue top hat, pointing his finger directly at passersby. Beneath his picture is the caption: "I WANT YOU FOR U.S. ARMY."[14] Over 4 million copies of this poster were printed during the war. Another highly effective recruiting poster had a wooden cross over an American soldier's grave. The caption read: "They invested everything—Their places must be filled."[15]

Posters also advertised war bonds (savings bonds that raised funds and kept inflation down) and liberty

http://www.library.georgetown.edu/dept/speccoll/n15.jpg - Microsoft Internet Explorer

File   Edit   View   Favorites   Tools   Help

Address http://www.library.georgetown.edu/dept/speccoll/n15.jpg

HALT the HUN!

First Call: American Posters of World War One, a Georgetown University Web site, features posters from the era that were designed to arouse patriotism and aid in the war effort. This one exhorts Americans to "Halt the Hun," or stop the Germans, by buying government bonds.

stamps to provide money for the war. One such poster pictured a demonic-looking German soldier carrying a blood-drenched bayonet. Its caption read: "Beat back the HUN with LIBERTY BONDS."[16] Still another showed a desperate mother protecting her baby. The caption read: "MUST CHILDREN DIE AND MOTHERS PLEAD IN VAIN? Buy More Liberty Bonds."[17]

To assure that European allies did not starve, America also launched a massive campaign to grow and conserve food. Posters urged Americans to eat less meat and to save or grow more food. One poster

Defeat the
KAISER *and*
his **U-BOATS**
V ctory Depends *on*
Which fails first,
food *or* frightfulness

Americans were also urged to conserve on food so that there would be enough to feed the troops abroad. This poster from the **World War I Poster Collection Guide** site asks Americans to eat less wheat to ensure victory over the Kaiser, Germany's leader.

showed a German watching a U-boat sink a ship. The poster's message asked Americans to conserve wheat so that more food could be sent to the troops.

Defeat the
KAISER and
his U-BOATS.
Victory depends on
which fails first, food or frightfulness.
Eat less WHEAT.[18]

"THE WAR TO END ALL WARS"

At the eleventh hour of the eleventh day of the eleventh month of the year 1918, the fighting in World War I came to an end. This is how the *New York Times* reported the armistice.

WITH THE AMERICAN ARMY IN FRANCE, Nov. 11— They [the soldiers on the western front] stopped fighting at 11 o'clock this morning. In a twinkling, four years of killing and massacre stopped as if God had swept His omnipotent finger across the scene of world carnage and had cried "Enough."[1]

Another *Times* journalist wrote:

Last night, for the first time since August in the first year of the war, there was no light of gunfire in the sky, no sudden stabs of flame through darkness, no spreading glow above black trees where for four years of nights human beings were smashed to death. The Fires of Hell had been put out.[2]

Colonel Thomas Gowenlock remembers the scene from his vantage point at the front:

All over the world on November 11, 1918, people were celebrating, dancing in the streets, drinking champagne, hailing the armistice that meant the end of the war. But at the front there was no celebration. Many soldiers believed the Armistice only a temporary measure and that the war would soon go on. As night came, the quietness, unearthly in its penetration, began to eat into their souls. The men sat around log fires, the first they had ever had at the front. They were trying to reassure themselves that there were no enemy [artillery] batteries . . . and no German bombing planes . . . [about to] blast them out of existence. They talked in low tones. They were nervous.

    After the long months of intense strain, . . . of thinking always in terms of war and the enemy, the abrupt release from it all was physical and psychological agony. Some suffered a total nervous collapse. Some . . . began to hope they would someday return to home and the embrace of loved ones. Some could think only of the crude little crosses that marked the graves of their comrades. Some fell into an exhausted sleep. All were bewildered by the sudden meaninglessness of their existence as soldiers. . . . What was to come next? They did not know—and hardly cared. Their minds were numbed by the shock of peace. [3]

Another American soldier, Sergeant Albert Haas, recalled how he felt that day:

I was glad. Glad that the war was over. . . . I though[t] of home and how the folks at home felt when they

received the same good news; of other folks whose loved ones would not come home, and what the stopping of fighting meant to them. It was the end of the most terrible four years of warfare the civilized world had ever known.[4]

Homecoming

The first troops to arrive home in 1919 were given heroes' welcomes. Big cities and small towns held victory parades, and as the troops marched down the streets in their uniforms, they were cheered by great crowds. Communities erected monuments to the dead and surviving veterans. The most famous monument built to commemorate those who died in World War I is the Tomb of the Unknown Soldier in Arlington National Cemetery, Virginia. In 1921, an unidentified World War I doughboy was buried there, and an honor guard was appointed to guard his grave. An inscription on the monument reads: "Here Rests In Honored Glory An American Soldier Known But To God."[5]

Armistice Day

On November 11, 1919, to mark the first anniversary of the armistice, President Woodrow Wilson issued a proclamation in remembrance of

Today in History: November 11

Access this Web site from http://www.myreportlinks.com

On November 11, 1918, Allied forces signed an armistice, or cease-fire agreement, with Germany, bringing an end to the fighting in World War I. Learn more about this day's observances throughout history on this Web site.

those who had given their lives in the war: "To us in America, the reflections of Armistice Day will be filled with solemn pride in the heroism of those who died in the country's service and with gratitude for the victory [in World War I]."[6] Armistice Day was observed as a holiday in many states beginning in the 1920s and 30s, but it did not become a federal holiday until 1938. Its focus was broadened—and its name changed to Veterans Day—in 1954 to remember those who had also served in World War II and the Korean War. Today, it honors the American veterans of all wars.

▷ Aftermath

After the parades were over, the troops coming home found that little had changed, and the future held little glory for them. Private Harold Dresser recalled:

> After the war was over I returned to my old job with the General Hardware Company and I've been there ever since. In my home town people point me out to strangers and say, "You'd never believe that fellow had a hat full of medals, would you?" And the strangers always say, no they never would.[7]

Life for the returning troops could be difficult. Some soldiers who had known the excitement of faraway places and the terror of trench warfare had a hard time readjusting to the quiet of civilian life.

For those who were seriously wounded in battle, who lost legs or arms or who were left with psychological illnesses, the adjustment was even more difficult. Some veterans of the Great War were never able to leave veterans' hospitals.

With the stock market crash of 1929, the decade-long Great Depression began. During the 1930s, some veterans, like many other Americans, found themselves without jobs, money, or homes. They demanded that the government pay them the cash bonus that they had been promised earlier. But with the federal government in financial trouble, Congress and President Herbert Hoover refused to pay the bonus.

▲ *The tents of Bonus Marchers line a field in Washington, D.C. These World War I veterans and their families descended upon the nation's capital in 1932 to demand payments promised them.*

In May 1932, nearly twenty thousand jobless and homeless veterans and their families, many of them catching rides in railroad freight cars, descended upon Washington, D.C. These men who had fought in France, many of whom were disabled, built a tent city, marched through Washington under American flags, and refused to leave without their bonuses. President Hoover ordered General Douglas MacArthur, a World War I veteran, to drive these veterans, who become known as the Bonus Marchers, from the capital. MacArthur's men, led by George Patton, another World War I veteran, attacked the Bonus Marchers from horseback with drawn swords, on foot with bayonets, and with tear gas. The troops set the tent city on fire. One Bonus Marcher and two veterans' babies died in the attack. Angry veterans screamed at the attacking troops, "Where were you in the [battle of the] Argonne, buddy?" but the troops did not listen.[8] The attack on the Bonus Marchers left many World War I veterans bitter and angry, wondering why they had fought so hard in France for a government that was now attacking them. Other veterans remained proud of their role in the Great War.

Was It Worth It?

President Woodrow Wilson went to France in 1919 with hopes of negotiating a peace that would not only make the world safe for democracy, but that would end all war. "Complete victory has brought

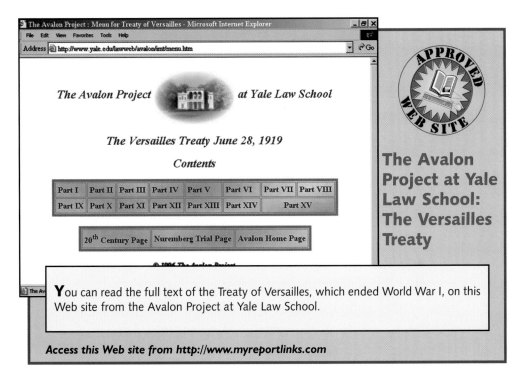

The Avalon Project : Menu for Treaty of Versailles - Microsoft Internet Explorer

File   Edit   View   Favorites   Tools   Help

Address http://www.yale.edu/lawweb/avalon/imt/menu.htm   Go

The Avalon Project   *at Yale Law School*

The Versailles Treaty June 28, 1919

Contents

Part I	Part II	Part III	Part IV	Part V	Part VI	Part VII	Part VIII
Part IX	Part X	Part XI	Part XII	Part XIII	Part XIV	Part XV	

20th Century Page	Nuremberg Trial Page	Avalon Home Page

© 1996 The Avalon Project

The Avalon Project at Yale Law School: The Versailles Treaty

You can read the full text of the Treaty of Versailles, which ended World War I, on this Web site from the Avalon Project at Yale Law School.

Access this Web site from http://www.myreportlinks.com

us, not peace alone, but the confident promise of a new day as well, in which justice shall replace force and jealous intrigue among the nations," said Wilson.[9]

Unfortunately, Britain, Italy, and especially France wanted to punish their foes. The Treaty of Versailles ignored most of Wilson's ideals. It deprived Germany of more than 10 percent of its 1914 territory (and 7 million of its people), and all of its colonies. It also required the payment of millions of dollars in reparations to the Allies, something that the starving and defeated Germans could not afford.

Though the Treaty of Versailles was a complex document, a cartoon from 1920 sums up its impact.

In it, the leaders of France, Britain, Italy, and the United States exit the great hall at Versailles after signing the treaty. A small child sobs nearby. A copy of the peace treaty lies beside the child, and a banner over his head reads: "1940 Class." The leaders are perplexed, and Premier Georges Clemenceau of France, known as the Tiger, says, "Curious! I seem to hear a child weeping!" The name of the cartoon is "Peace and Future Cannon Fodder."[10] The cartoon proved prophetic: Millions of children in 1919 would grow up to fight on the battlefields of World War II only twenty years later.

Certainly the seeds of World War II were sown in the trenches of World War I. An embittered German Army corporal who had fought on the western front

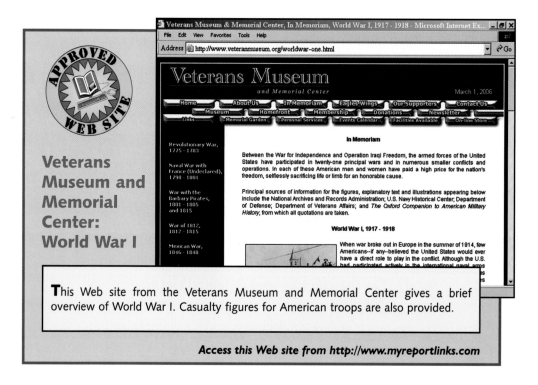

Veterans Museum and Memorial Center: World War I

This Web site from the Veterans Museum and Memorial Center gives a brief overview of World War I. Casualty figures for American troops are also provided.

Access this Web site from http://www.myreportlinks.com

PEACE AND FUTURE CANNON FODDER

The Tiger: "Curious! I seem to hear a child weeping!"

▲ Will Dyson's "Peace and Future Cannon Fodder."

would come to shape the future of the world based upon his experiences in the Great War. That soldier, Adolf Hitler, was appalled by Germany's surrender in 1918 and believed that Germany had been betrayed by its politicians. Hitler also demanded that the wrongs done to Germany by the Treaty of Versailles be righted—even if that meant another war. Adolf Hitler led his nation into World War II little more than twenty years after World War I, "the war to end all wars," had ceased.

The Internet sites described below can be accessed at http://www.myreportlinks.com

▶ **The Great War and the Shaping of the 20th Century**
Editor's Choice Learn about WWI, the Great War, from this PBS Web site.

▶ **Dear Home: Letters From WWI**
Editor's Choice View World War I letters on this History Channel Web site.

▶ **The Price of Freedom: Americans at War**
Editor's Choice View World War I artifacts from the National Museum of American History.

▶ **The World War I Document Archive**
Editor's Choice This site includes a collection of documents related to the First World War.

▶ **The *Stars and Stripes:* The American Soldiers' Newspaper**
Editor's Choice Read a newspaper published for American soldiers during World War I.

▶ **On The Homefront: America During World War I and World War II**
Editor's Choice This site provides resources on the war effort at home during both world wars.

▶ **The Aerodrome: Aces and Aircraft of World War I**
Learn more about the flying aces and aircraft of World War I.

▶ **American Leaders Speak: Recordings From World War I and the 1920 Election**
Listen to audio clips from American leaders during and just after the war.

▶ **Anonymous Diary, September 18, 1918–July 20, 1919**
Read this diary account on the Women Veterans Historical Collection Web site.

▶ **The Avalon Project at Yale Law School: The Versailles Treaty**
The text of the Treaty of Versailles is presented on this Web site.

▶ **Battle Lines: Letters From America's Wars**
This Web site contains a sampling of letters written by American soldiers.

▶ **Digitized Primary American History Sources**
View a collection of primary sources of American history.

▶ **First Call: American Posters of World War One**
View Georgetown University's collection of World War I posters.

▶ **FirstWorldWar.com**
Learn about World War I from this comprehensive Web site.

▶ **The First World War: Sources for History**
Learn about World War I through the National Archives of Great Britain.

Report Links

The Internet sites described below can be accessed at
http://www.myreportlinks.com

▶ **The Florida Memory Project: World War I Service Cards**
View the service cards for American troops from Florida.

▶ **Historic American Sheet Music**
View Duke University's collection of historic sheet music on this site.

▶ **Learning Curve: The Great War, 1914 to 1918**
Take a look at World War I from the British perspective.

▶ **Lost Poets of the Great War**
Read about some of the poets of World War I who lost their lives in combat.

▶ **Named Campaigns—World War I**
The Army's Center of Military History gives an overview of World War I battles.

▶ **Newspaper Pictorials: World War I Rotogravures**
View newspaper images from World War I on this site.

▶ **Our Documents: President Woodrow Wilson's Fourteen Points**
Read President Woodrow Wilson's Fourteen Points, his plan for world peace.

▶ **Our Documents: Zimmermann Telegram**
View the telegram that enraged American public opinion and helped lead America into war.

▶ **Today in History: November 11**
The historical significance of November 11 is the focus of this Library of Congress site.

▶ **U.S. Centennial of Flight Commission: The Flying Aces of World War I**
Learn about the "flying aces" of World War I on this Web site.

▶ **Veterans History Project**
This Library of Congress site presents first-person accounts of American veterans.

▶ **Veterans Museum and Memorial Center: World War I**
Read a brief overview of the war on this Web site dedicated to veterans.

▶ **Wars and Conflict: World War One**
Read articles about World War I on this BBC Web site.

▶ **World War One**
Maps showing World War I campaigns can be found on this West Point Web site.

▶ **World War I Poster Collection Guide**
This college Web site offers a collection of World War I posters.

annex—To take over the territory of another nation without war.

armistice—A truce or cease-fire in a war.

conscientious objector—Someone who refuses to fight in a war because he or she feels war is immoral or contrary to his or her beliefs.

conscription—Required service in the military.

depth charges—Explosives dropped into the ocean to sink submarines.

destroyers—Surface ships that fight submarines.

doughboys—The nickname for American soldiers serving in World War I.

draft—An order to join the armed services in time of war.

eastern front—The battle line between Germany and Russia in World War I.

Fourteen Points—President Woodrow Wilson's peace plan.

gangrene—An infection common among wounded World War I soldiers forced to wait long hours for aid. If too serious, gangrene required that the soldier's wounded limb be amputated.

going over the top—Leaving a trench to rush into no-man's-land to attack an enemy trench.

mobilization—The readying of an army for war.

no-man's-land—The shell hole and barbwire-covered wasteland between the trenches.

outflank—To maneuver around one side of an enemy army.

poison gas—Airborne chemicals used in World War I to blind or suffocate troops to death.

propaganda—Facts, ideas, rumors, or exaggerations presented as fact that are used in support of a particular point of view or against an opponent's cause.

reparations—Money paid by one nation to another for causing harm during a war. Germany had to pay large reparations after World War I.

rolling barrage—A wave of artillery fire that moves just ahead of advancing troops.

shrapnel—Pieces of an exploding artillery shell.

stevedores—Dockworkers who unload ships.

suffragist—A person seeking suffrage, or the right to vote. The term *suffragist* usually applies to a woman seeking the vote for women, denied until 1920.

U-boat—A German submarine.

unrestricted submarine warfare—A German policy of sinking any ship in the war zone suspected of bringing supplies to Britain.

western front—The battle line between the troops of Germany and those of Britain, France, and the United States.

zeppelin—Large German motorized airships that dropped bombs on England during the war.

Chapter 1. The Battle for Belleau Wood

1. Frank Freidel, *Over There: The Story of America's First Great Overseas Crusade* (New Jersey: Burford Books, 1964), p. 122. Reprinted by permission of Burford Books, Inc. from OVER THERE by Frank Freidel, copyright © 1964 by Frank Freidel.

2. "A Letter Describing the BATTLE for BELLEAU WOOD by Lieutenant H.R. Long USMC," *THE ADIRONDACK ENTERPRISE,* Saranac Lake, New York, Friday, August 23, 1918.

3. Alvin M. Josephy, Jr., ed., *The American Heritage History of World War I* (New York: American Heritage Publishing Company, 1964), p. 280.

4. Freidel, p. 137.

5. Ibid.

6. Ibid., pp. 137, 140.

7. "A Letter Describing the BATTLE for BELLEAU WOOD."

8. Freidel, p. 143.

9. Ibid.

10. Ibid., pp. 143–144.

11. Josephy, p. 283.

Chapter 2. A Brief History of World War I

1. World War I Document Archive, Brigham Young University Library, "The Assassination of Archduke Franz Ferdinand," p. 2, n.d., <http://www.lib.byu.edu/~rdh/wwi/1914/ferddead.html> (November 15, 2005).

2. PBS, *Freedom: A History of US,* "Archduke Franz Ferdinand: An Eyewitness Account by Count Franz von Harrach," n.d., <http://www.pbs.org/wnet/historyofus/web11/features /source/docs/C04.pdf> (November 15, 2005).

3. World War I Document Archive, Brigham Young University Library, "The Assassination of Archduke Franz Ferdinand."

4. John T. Cushing and Arthur F. Stone, eds., *Vermont in the World War, 1917–1919* (Vermont: Vermont Legislature, 1928), p. 429.

5. Mildred Aldrich, *A Hilltop on the Marne: Being Letters Written June 3–September 8, 1914,* Part V. Letter of July 30, 1914. Project Gutenberg e-Book, n.d., <http://www.gutenberg.org /files/11011/11011-h/11011-h.htm> (November 8, 2005).

6. Edward Jablonski, *A Pictorial History of the World War I Years* (New York: Doubleday and Company, 1979), p. 27.

7. Ibid., p. 33.

8. Military.com, "Letter from Otto Luening in Germany to Karl Wagner in the United States," August 27, 1914," pp. 1–2, <http://www.military.com/Content/MoreContent?file=luening01> (November 15, 2005).

9. Mildred Aldrich, *A Hilltop on the Marne: Being Letters Written June 3–September 8, 1914,* Part XIII. Letter of September 8, 1914. Project Gutenberg e-Book, <http://www.gutenberg.org/files/11011/11011-h/11011-h.htm> (November 8, 2005).

10. Paul Fussell, *The Great War and Modern Memory* (London: Oxford University Press, 1975), p. 29.

11. John Ellis, *Eye-Deep in Hell: Trench Warfare in World War I* (Baltimore: Johns Hopkins University Press, 1976), p. 94.

12. Alvin M. Josephy, Jr., ed., *The American Heritage History of World War I* (New York: American Heritage Publishing Company, 1964), p. 185.

13. World War I Document Archive, Brigham Young University Library, "Stirring Scenes When Great Liner Went to Bottom," the *Washington Post,* Tuesday, May 11, 1915, p. 10.

14. Josephy, p. 204.

15. Ibid.

16. Ibid., p. 205.

17. *The H. G. Wells Conservatory: A Very Comprehensive List of Books Written by H. G. Wells,* compiled by Geoffrey Doyle, p. 3, n.d., <http://www.cs.clemson.edu/~tdoyle/hgbib.html> (November 15, 2005).

18. Fussell, p. 32.

Chapter 3. Soldiers' Stories

1. Frank Freidel, *Over There: The Story of America's First Great Overseas Crusade* (New Jersey: Burford Books, 1964), pp. 11–12. Reprinted by permission of Burford Books, Inc. from OVER THERE by Frank Freidel, copyright © 1964 by Frank Freidel.

2. The Doughboy Center, Partnership of the Veterans History Program of the Library of Congress and the Great War Society, "Second Army. In Their Own Words, Part Two," p. 2, n.d., <http://www.worldwar1.com/dbc/ow_2.htm> (November 15, 2005).

3. The Doughboy Center, "The Origins of Doughboy," pp. 4–5, n.d., <http://www.worldwar1.com/dbc/origindb.htm> (November 15, 2005).

4. The Doughboy Center, "In Their Own Words, Part Two," p. 5, n.d., <http://www.worldwar1.com/dbc/ow_2.htm> (November 15, 2005).

5. Ibid., p. 6

6. Ibid.

7. Library of Congress, American Memory, *American Life Histories: Manuscripts from the Federal Writers Project, 1936–1940,* "Great Lakes Folklore: S.J. Premo," p. 5, <http://memory.loc.gov /ammem/wpaintro/wpahome.html> (November 15, 2005).

8. The Doughboy Center, "In Their Own Words, Part Three," pp. 1–2, n.d., <http://www.worldwar1.com/dbc/ow_3.htm> (November 15, 2005).

9. Ibid., p. 2.

10. The Doughboy Center, "In Their Own Words, Part Two," pp. 7–8.

11. Ibid., pp. 8–9.

12. The History Channel, "Dear Home—Letters from WWI," Letter from Edward Luckert, July 22, 1918, pp.1–2, <http://www .historychannel.com/letters/edward_luckert.html> (November 15, 2005).

13. The Doughboy Center, "In Their Own Words, Part Three," pp. 4–5.

14. The History Channel, "Dear Home—Letters from WWI," Letter from Albert Smith, October 15, 1918, pp. 1–2, <http:// www.historychannel.com/letters/albert_smith.html> (November 15, 2005).

15. The History Channel, "Dear Home—Letters from WWI," Letter from Stull Holt, September 1, 1917, p. 2, <http://www .historychannel.com/letters/stull_holt.html> (November 15, 2005).

16. The Doughboy Center, "In Their Own Words, Part Seven," pp. 2–3, n.d., <http://www.worldwar1.com/dbc/ow_7.htm> (November 15 2005).

17. The Doughboy Center, "In Their Own Words, Part Five," p. 3, n.d., <http://www.worldwar1.com/dbc/ow_5.htm> (November 15, 2005).

18. Library of Congress, American Memory, *American Life Histories: Manuscripts from the Federal Writers Project, 1936–1940,* "Andrew Johnson," p. 3, n.d., <http://memory.loc.gov/ammem /ndlpedu/features/timeline/progress/wwone/mybit.html> (November 15, 2005).

19. PBS, *American Experience—War Letters,* Featured Letters: Lewis Plush, n.d., <http://www.pbs.org/wgbh/amex/warletters /letters/warletter_22.html> (November 15, 2005).

Chapter 4. Above the Lines, Behind the Lines, and After the War

1. World War I Document Archive, Brigham Young University Library, "Long Expected Airship Raid," the *Fort Wayne Daily News,* Wednesday, January 20, 1915, p. 16.

2. W. Kevin Durden, The United States Air Force, *Aerospace Power Journal,* "World War I from the Viewpoint of American Airmen," p. 2, September 1988, <http://www.airpower.maxwell .af.mil/airchronicles/apj/apj88/durden.html> (November 15, 2005).

3. Eddie Rickenbacker, *Fighting the Flying Circus,* "Lufbury Is Killed," n.d., <http://www.richthofen.com/rickenbacker/> (November 15, 2005).

4. Frank Freidel, *Over There: The Story of America's First Great Overseas Crusade* (New Jersey: Burford Books, 1964), p. 81. Reprinted by permission of Burford Books, Inc. from OVER THERE by Frank Freidel, copyright © 1964 by Frank Freidel.

5. Dr. William Chaikin, "Quartermaster Supply in the AEF, 1917–1918," *Quartermaster Review,* May–June 1950, Army Quartermaster Foundation, Inc., <http://www.qmfound.com /supply_aef.htm> (November 15, 2005).

6. The University of Kansas, Online Library, Documents of World War I, *The Medical History of WWI, Nursing Documents, Nellie Fairchild Rote,* "Nurse Helen Fairchild, My Aunt, My Hero," p. 5, n.d., <http://www.ku.edu/carrie/specoll/medical//MaMh /MyAunt.htm> (November 15, 2005).

7. The History Channel, "Dear Home—Letters from World War I," Letter from Marion Rice, January 3, 1917, p. 2, <http://www.historychannel.com/letters/marion_rice.html> (November 15, 2005).

8. Freidel, p. 78.

9. U.S. Senate Historical Office, "September 30, 1918—A Vote for Women," n.d., <http://www.senate.gov/artandhistory /history/minute/A_Vote_For_Women.htm> (November 15, 2005).

10. Freidel, p. 254.

11. Ibid., p. 256.

12. Ibid., p. 252.

13. Ibid., p. 256.

14. Ibid., p. 262.

Chapter 5. The War at Home

1. World War I Document Archive, Brigham Young University Library, Woodrow Wilson, *War Messages,* 65th Congress, 1st Session, Senate Document No. 5, Serial No. 7264, Washington, D.C., 1917, pp. 3–8, <http://www.lib.byu.edu/~rdh/wwi/1917 /wilswarm.html> (November 15, 2005).

2. Howard Zinn, *A People's History of the United States* (New York: Harper & Row, 1980), p. 355.

3. Eugene V. Debs Internet Archive, "The Canton, Ohio, Speech," p. 7, 1918, <http://www.marxists.org/archive/debs /works/1918/canton.htm> (November 15, 2005).

4. World War I Document Archive, Brigham Young University Library, *United States Statutes at Large,* Washington, D.C., 1918, vol. XL, pp. 553 ff, *A portion of the amendment to Section 3 of the Espionage Act of June 15, 1917,* <http://www.lib.byu.edu/~rdh /wwi/1918/usspy.html> (November 15, 2005).

5. Zinn, p. 362.

6. History Matters, The U.S. Survey Course on the Web, "Four Minute Men: Volunteer Speeches During World War I— Speech by a Four Minute Man," October 8, 1917, <http:// historymatters.gmu.edu/d/4970/> (November 15, 2005).

7. Library of Congress, American Memory, *American Life Histories: Manuscripts from the Federal Writers Project, 1936–1940,* "Reminiscences of a Rebel," n.d. <http://memory.loc.gov/learn /features/timeline/progress/wwone/rebel.html> (January 4, 2006).

8. Library of Congress, American Memory, *American Life Histories: Manuscripts from the Federal Writers Project, 1936–1940,* Frank Vanderlip, "One Hundred Million Soldiers," <http:// memory.loc.gov/learn/features/timeline/progress/wwone/soldiers. html> (January 4, 2006).

9. Library of Congress, American Memory, *American Life Histories: Manuscripts from the Federal Writers Project, 1936–1940,* Frank Boyd, "Harlem Rent Parties," n.d., <http://memory .loc.gov/learn/features/timeline/progress/prohib/rent.html> (January 4, 2006).

10. Library of Congress, American Memory, *American Life Histories: Manuscripts from the Federal Writers Project, 1936–1940,* Charles Fusco, "Italian Munitions Worker," n.d., <http://memory loc.gov/ammem/ndlpedu/features/timeline/progress/wwone /munition.html> (January 4, 2006).

11. Tae H. Kim, Pacific Northwest Labor History Projects, "Where Women Worked During World War I," n.d., <http://faculty.washington.edu/gregoryj/strike/kim.htm> (January 4, 2006).

12. Harriot Stanton Blatch, *Mobilizing Woman-Power,* Project Gutenberg eBook, Chapter VI, "Women Over the Top in America," pp. 29–30, n.d., <http://www.gutenberg.org/files/10080/10080-h/10080-h.htm#VI> (January 4, 2006).

13. National Archives and Records Administration, Charters of Freedom—Constitution of the United States, Amendments 11 to 27, n.d., <http://www.archives.gov/national-archives-experience/charters/constitution_amendments_11-27.html> (January 4, 2006).

14. Nate Williams, "German-Americans in World War I," Wittenberg University, pp. 5–6, n.d., <http://www.wfa-usa.org/new/germanamer.htm> (January 4, 2006).

15. Ibid., p. 4.

Chapter 6. The War in Song and Literature

1. History Matters, The U.S. Survey Course on the Web, "I Didn't Raise My Boy to Be a Soldier": Singing Against the War, n.d., http://historymatters.gmu.edu/d/4942/ pp. 1–2 (January 4, 2006).

2. Aftermath, "Over There: The Story of America's Most Popular World War I Song," pp. 1–2, n.d., <http://www.aftermathww1.com/overthere.asp> (January 4, 2006).

3. Aftermath, "Keep the Home Fires Burning," p. 1, n.d., <http://www.aftermathww1.com/homefires.asp> (January 4, 2006).

4. The Industrial Workers of the World, "Don't Take My Papa Away From Me," pp. 1–2, n.d., <http://www.fortunecity.com/tinpan/parton/2/donttake.html> (January 4, 2006).

5. The Doughboy Center, "Lieutenant James Reese Europe Songs Brought Back From the Battlefield," pp. 5–6, <http://www.worldwar1.com/sfjre.htm> (January 4, 2006).

6. Frank Freidel, *Over There: The Story of America's First Great Overseas Crusade* (New Jersey: Burford Books, 1964), p. viii. Reprinted by permission of Burford Books, Inc. from OVER THERE by Frank Freidel, copyright © 1964 by Frank Freidel.

7. Emory University, *Lost Poets of the Great War,* "Alan Seeger," pp. 1–2, n.d., <http://www.english.emory.edu/LostPoets/Seeger.html> (January 4, 2006).

8. The Doughboy Center, "John Allan Wyeth" p. 10, n.d., <http://www.worldwar1.com/sfwyeth.htm#lv> (January 4, 2006).

9. Emmett J. Scott, *Scott's Official History of the American Negro in the World War,* 1919, p. 322, <http://www.gwpda.org/wwi-www/Scott/SCh22.htm> (January 4, 2006).

10. W. Kevin Durden, The United States Air Force, *Aerospace Power Journal,* "World War I From the Viewpoint of American Airmen," Summer 1988, <http://www.airpower.maxwell.af.mil/airchronicles/apj/apj88/durden.html> (January 4, 2006).

11. Erich Maria Remarque, *All Quiet on the Western Front* (Boston: Little, Brown and Company, 1929), p. 88.

12. Ibid., p. 226.

13. Ernest Hemingway, *A Farewell to Arms* (New York: Charles Scribner's Sons, 1929), p. 118.

14. Ibid., pp. 184–185.

Chapter 7. Press Coverage and Propaganda

1. World War I Document Archive, Brigham Young University Library, "9–10 June, 1918: The Americans Take Belleau Wood," p. 1, <http://www.lib.byu.edu/~rdh/wwi/1918/belleau.html> (January 4, 2006).

2. The *Washington Post,* Sunday, August 4, 1918, p. 9.

3. Ibid., p. 1.

4. Ibid.

5. Ibid., p. 2.

6. Ibid., p. 5.

7. Ibid., p. 17.

8. Ibid., p. 16.

9. Rebecca Zurier, *Art for the Masses: A Radical Magazine and Its Graphics, 1911–1917* (Philadelphia: Temple University Press, 1988), p. 60.

10. Michigan State University Library, the *Masses,* Cover, November 1914, <http://www.lib.msu.edu/coll/main/spec_col/radicalism/exhibits/masses/images/14novc.jpg> (January 4, 2006).

11. Rebecca Zurier, p. 22.

12. Harry Weinberger, "Gone to Jail," *Mother Earth Bulletin,* vol. 1, no. 5, February 1919, Anarchist Archives, n.d., <http://dwardmac.pitzer.edu/Anarchist_Archives/goldman/ME/mebv1n5.html> (January 4, 2006).

13. Philip Randolph, the *Messenger,* July 1918.

14. The Library of Congress, Information Bulletin, "John Bull and Uncle Sam," November 1999, <http://www.loc.gov/loc/lcib/9911/bullsam.html> (January 4, 2006).

15. Tutt Library, Colorado College, "World War I Poster Collection U.S. Recruitment Miscellaneous," Poster #122, n.d., <http://www.coloradocollege.edu/library/SpecialCollections/HistoricalCollections/WWI/RM122.html> (January 4, 2006).

16. Tutt Library, Colorado College, "World War I Poster Collection U.S. Liberty Bonds," Poster #249, n.d., <http://www.coloradocollege.edu/library/SpecialCollections/HistoricalCollections/WWI/LB240-254.html> (January 4, 2006).

17. Ibid, Poster #253.

18. Tutt Library, Colorado College, "World War I Poster Collection U.S. Food Administration," Poster #014, n.d., <http://www.coloradocollege.edu/library/SpecialCollections/HistoricalCollections/WWI/FA014.html> (January 4, 2006).

Chapter 8. "The War to End All Wars"

1. World War I Document Archive, Brigham Young University Library, "9-11, November 1918, *The New York Times* Reports the End of the War," <http://www.lib.byu.edu/~rdh/wwi/1918/nytend.html> (January 4, 2006).

2. Ibid.

3. Thomas R. Gowenlock, *Soldiers of Darkness* (1936), reprinted in Paul M. Angle, *The American Reader* (New York: Rand McNally & Company, 1958), p. 504.

4. The Doughboy Center, "In Their Own Words, Part Seven," p. 10, n.d., <http://www.worldwar1.com/dbc/ow_7.htm> (January 4, 2006).

5. The Doughboy Center, "America's Unknown Soldier," p. 1, n.d., <http://www.worldwar1.com/dbc/unksold.htm> (January 4, 2006).

6. Miami-Dade County Public Schools, Patriotism.org, "Veteran's Day," p. 1, n.d., <http://www.patriotism.org/veterans_day/> (January 4, 2006).

7. The Doughboy Center, "In Their Own Words, Part Seven," p. 15.

8. William Manchester, *The Glory and the Dream: A Narrative History of America, 1932–1972* (New York: Bantam Books, 1974), p. 14.

9. Pilgrim Hall Museum, "Thanksgiving Day–1918, By The President of the United States of American—A Proclamation," <http://www.pilgrimhall.org/ThanxProc1910.htm> (January 4, 2006).

10. Will Dyson, "Peace and Future Cannon Fodder," *Daily Herald,* London, England, May 17, 1919.

Allan, Tony. *The Causes of World War I.* Chicago: Heinemann Library, 2003.

Barber, Nicola. *World War I: The Western Front.* Mankato, Minn.: Smart Apple Media, 2003.

Grant, Reg. *Armistice, 1918.* Austin, Tex.: Raintree Steck-Vaughn, 2001.

Hamilton, John. *Battles of World War I.* Edina, Minn.: ABDO & Daughters, 2004.

Hansen, Ole Steen. *The War in the Trenches.* Austin, Tex.: Raintree Steck-Vaughn, 2001.

Holden, Henry M. *Woodrow Wilson.* Berkeley Heights, N.J.: MyReportLinks.com Books, 2003.

Preston, Diana. *Remember the Lusitania.* New York: Walker & Company, 2003.

Ross, Stewart. *Leaders of World War I.* Austin, Tex.: Raintree Steck-Vaughn, 2003.

Ruggiero, Adriane. *World War I.* Tarrytown, N.Y.: Benchmark Books, 2003.

White, Matt. *Cameras on the Battlefield: Photos of War.* Mankato, Minn.: Capstone Press, 2002.

Zeinert, Karen. *Those Extraordinary Women of World War I.* Brookfield, Conn.: Millbrook Press, 2001.

Fiction

Hemingway, Ernest. *A Farewell to Arms.* New York: Charles Scribner's Sons, 1929.

Remarque, Erich Maria. *All Quiet on the Western Front.* Boston: Little, Brown and Company, 1929.